Calling
the Shots

Other Books on Film, Radio Drama, and Broadcasting
from Quarry Press

Best Canadian Screenplays
edited by Douglas Bowie and Tom Shoebridge

All the Bright Company:
Radio Drama Produced by Andrew Allan
edited by Howard Fink and John Jackson

Words on Waves: Selected Radio Plays of Earle Birney

Beyond the Printed Word:
The Evolution of Canada's Broadcast News Heritage
edited by Richard Lochead

Calling
the Shots

PROFILES OF
WOMEN
FILMMAKERS

BY
Janis Cole
AND
Holly Dale

Quarry Press

The publisher gratefully acknowledges the assistance of The Canada Council, the Ontario Arts Council, the Department of Communications, and the Ontario Publishing Centre.

Canadian Cataloguing in Publication Data

    Calling the shots: profiles of women filmmakers

ISBN 1-55082-085-0

    1. Women motion picture producers and directors — Interviews.
I. Cole, Janis   II. Dale, Holly.

PN1995.9.W6D35 1993   791.43'023'0922   C93-090516-4

Cover photograph of Julie Dash by Floyd Webb, courtesy of Julie Dash; photograph of Deepa Mehta by Kerry Hayes, courtesy of Shaftesbury Films; photograph of Mira Nair by Mitch Epstein, courtesy of Samuel Goldwyn; photograph of Particia Rozema by Caroline Benjo, courtesy of Alliance Releasing; photograph of Penelope Spheeris by Garry Farr, courtesy of New Century/Vista Film Co.; photograph of Sandy Wilson by Alex Dukay, courtesy of Alliance Releasing.

Design Consultant: Keith Abraham.
Typeset by Quarry Press, Inc.
Printed and bound in Canada by Webcom Limited, Toronto, Ontario.

Published by Quarry Press, Inc.,
P.O. Box 1061, Kingston, Ontario K7L 4Y5.

For Barry Cole (1952-1991)

and for our fathers:
Victor John Cole (1924-1990) &
Roland Basil Dale (1930-1991)

They gave us our fierce sense
of independence,
and a strong sense of self.

CONTENTS

Holly Dale and Janis Cole

Acknowledgements

The making of our film *Calling the Shots* provided us with an opportunity to interview many of the directors included in these pages. We are grateful to all of the directors who generously gave of their time and shared their experiences with us, both for the film and for this book.

The people who responded to our film by telling us that it empowered and encouraged them — your words did the same for us when we undertook the writing of this book.

For providing financial support to make this book possible, we would like to thank The Canada Council (Explorations Program), Toronto Arts Council (Assistance to Writers), and Ontario Arts Council (Writer's Reserve Fund). We are also very grateful to each publisher who considered our manuscript and recommended that it receive Writer's Reserve funding.

Many friends encouraged this creative endeavor and supported us when we were in need of a refreshing break from our computers. We'd especially like to thank Kay Armatage, Rose Close Baldwin, Linda Beath, Colin Campell, Susan Feldman, Lynne Fernie, Sylvia Fraser, Rina Fraticelli, Michael Hollet, Johanna Householder, Zuhair Kashmeri, Debra Henderson, Alice Klein, Shelley Malonowich, Leeann Markle, David McIlwraith, Heather Mitchell, Colleen Murphy, Anne Sinclair, Lori Spring, Lisa Tremblay, Joanne Vannicola, and John Walker for their warmth, love, and friendship throughout this project.

Our mothers are always supportive of our undertakings, and encourage us to express ourselves and our viewpoints, as our fathers did when they were alive. We are especially proud of them, not only for loving us as their children, but for loving us completely.

And finally, our deepest thanks to Julie Martin, for countless hours of assistance with the additional research, typing, layout, and production of the manuscript. We couldn't have done it without your valuable help, Julie!

Photo Credits

We are grateful to the directors in this book who provided photographs of themselves. Likewise, we wish to thank Alliance Releasing, the National Film Board of Canada, the New Century/Vista Film Company, *NOW Magazine*, Samuel Goldwyn, the Toronto Festival of Festivals, Irene Grainger, Suzie King, Rafy, and Paul Till for their assistance in providing additional courtesy stills. We appreciate all of the photographs that have been contributed to us, and regret that when the photographer's name has not been supplied, we are only able to credit the source.

Holly Dale and Janis Cole, p. 8, by John Walker. *Ida Lupino*, p. 13, courtesy of Ida Lupino. *Karen Arthur*, p. 17, by Janis Cole; p. 27, courtesy of Karen Arthur. *Lizzie Borden*, p. 31, by Paul Till; p. 37, by Janis Cole. *Martha Coolidge*, p. 41 and p. 51, courtesy of Martha Coolidge. *Julie Dash*, p. 57, by Monika Nikore, courtesy of Julie Dash; p. 63, courtesy of Julie Dash. *Jill Godmilow*, p. 69 and p. 77, courtesy of Jill Godmilow. *Lee Grant*, p. 83, by Rafy, courtesy of the Toronto Festival of Festivals (TFF). *Randa Haines*, p. 95, by Janis Cole; p. 101, courtesy of Randa Haines. *Amy Heckerling*, p. 107 and p. 113, courtesy of Amy Heckerling. *Micheline Lanctôt*, p. 119 and p. 127, courtesy of the National Film Board of Canada (NFB). *Deepa Mehta*, p. 133, courtesy of Deepa Mehta; p. 139, by Kerry Hayes, courtesy of Shaftesbury Films. *Mira Nair*, p. 143, by Rafy, courtesy of TFF; p. 151, courtesy of Mira Nair. *Euzhane Palcy*, p. 155, by Tom Kim, courtesy of TFF; p. 161, courtesy of Euzhane Palcy. *Lea Pool*, p. 163, and p. 169, courtesy of the NFB. *Patricia Rozema*, p. 173, by Rafy, courtesy of TFF; p. 181, by Caroline Benjo. *Susan Seidelman*, p. 187, by John Clifford, courtesy of Susan Seidelman; p. 195, courtesy of Susan Seidelman. *Joan Micklin Silver*, p. 203 and p. 209, courtesy of Joan Micklin Silver. *Penelope Spheeris*, p. 215, by Susie King; p. 221, by Garry Farr, courtesy of New Century/Vista Film Company. *Joan Tewkesbury*, p. 227, by Janis Cole; p. 233, courtesy of Joan Tewkesbury. *Anne Wheeler*, p. 239, by Nancy Ackerman, courtesy of TTF; p. 245, courtesy of the NFB. *Sandy Wilson*, p. 249, by Ronny Shinder, courtesy of TTF; p. 255, by Janis Cole.

Preface

There are two reasons why we decided to write this book. First, while there are many anthologies available that have presented the viewpoints of men who direct films, we have never found a similar collection that presents the personal accounts of women filmmakers. At best, one or two women have been included in a book that examines twenty or more men who work in the film industry. Upon discovering this, we felt a strong urge and necessity to fill that void in cinema literature. Second, while there are several books that examine feminist film theory, primarily through the analysis of women's on-screen image, or an analysis of alternative filmmakers working in avant-garde, documentary, counter cinema, or feminist film, we haven't seen any books that present a collection of contemporary viewpoints from a wide variety of woman filmmakers, both mainstream and marginal.

Some people would argue, why a book about women? After all women have now made it in the film industry. Others would strongly disagree, feeling that special attention is still needed around funding, work opportunities, and exhibition. It's true that some of the top grossing films in the last few years have been directed by women (*Look Who's Talking* and *Wayne's World*), but at the same time the number of women who are directing films in North America is miniscule when compared to the number of men.

Since feature film directing in a male dominated industry is extremely difficult for women who want to maintain their own vision, the investigation into how women are able to do that became important for us to explore.

In our book we attempt to present a full range of views by documenting both the accomplishments and struggles of today's women directors, told through their own personal accounts. Due to limited space, it is impossible to include all of the women directing films world-wide in just one book. So we decided to focus on North American women working in the feature film industry today. Even at that we are not able to include everyone, so in our selection we try to present a cross section that is representative of contemporary women directors working in Canada and the United States. All of the women included in this anthology have directed at least one feature drama, and most of them have worked long enough that they've amassed a wealth of experience through the many different passages in their film careers. For example, Sandy Wilson, Mira Nair, Lea Pool, Martha Coolidge, Anne Wheeler, and Lee Grant have extensive credentials not only in drama, but also have substantial credits in documentary filmmaking. Penelope Spheeris directed rock videos before moving into dramatic filmmaking. Joan Micklin Silver made educational films, Randa Haines worked in continuity, Patrica Rozema was an assistant director, Karen Arthur worked in the camera department, and Jill Godmilow was an editor.

Our initial interest to delve into the topic of women directors grew from our own experiences as independent filmmakers in Canada over the past seventeen years. Our body of work is primarily documentary, and in 1988 we completed a feature length film entitled *Calling the Shots*. The film profiles Canadian, American and International women filmmakers, and to the best of our knowledge is the first compilation film of its kind.

During the three year period that we worked on *Calling the Shots*, we spoke with such experts as Kathleen Shannon, the founder of Studio "D" of the National Film Board of Canada; Molly Haskell, author of *From Reverence to Rape*; Kay Armatage, a filmmaker, professor, and Chair of Women's Studies at the University of Toronto; independent producer and former head of Telefilm Canada Linda Beath; and film critic Karen Jaehne.

We also conducted over fifty interviews on film, accumulated research on more than ninety female filmmakers, and viewed over one hundred and fifty films made by women. We amassed a wealth of valuable material that was impossible to weave into the structure of the film. That did not diminish the value of the many stories and experiences that we had to leave out; rather, it left us looking for another way to share them.

When *Calling the Shots* was completed and we began screening it for audiences, we received feedback that the film was both inspirational and encouraging. Many viewers vowed that they would follow their dreams with a stronger determination after seeing our film. It was then that we realized how many artists,

Ida Lupino: The Mother of Us All

especially women, were looking for this type of creative insight, providing them with role models in film and valuable resource material about the industry.

The fact that we had a surplus of interesting material left over from the film, combined with our knowledge of how few resources were available, made us realize that we could present the challenging insights of women directors to an even greater number of people by communicating their stories in another format. So we decided to begin once again the journey of exploring the uncensored, innovative, and controversial ideas of some of today's most prolific female image makers — this time in a book.

The book consists of compelling interviews illustrating personal portraits of twenty women directors in North America. Each portrait is preceded by a comprehensive summary of the filmmaker's career and work in film. Also included is a filmography on each filmmaker which lists title, year of release, and production company.

The bulk of the conversations are derived from the existing transcripts of interviews conducted for the film *Calling the Shots*. In addition, since artists are always evolving, changing moment to moment, film to film, we have contacted some of the filmmakers for updates and additional comments on their most recent projects.

Since the making of *Calling the Shots*, Amy Heckerling has directed the blockbuster hits *Look Who's Talking* and *Look Who's Talking Too*; Euzhane Palcy released her expose of South Africa *A Dry White Season*; Anne Wheeler gained critical acclaim with *Bye Bye Blues*; and Sandy Wilson went from the critics' warm embrace of *My American Cousin* to the cool reception of *American Boyfriends*.

There are also several new filmmakers that have emerged into the feature film arena in the past few years that we've included: Mira Nair (*Salaam Bombay!*, *Mississippi Masala*); Julie Dash (*Daughters of the Dust*); and in Canada directors Patricia Rozema (*I've Heard the Mermaids Singing* and *White Room*) and Deepa Mehta (*Sam and Me* and *Camilla*).

The conversations that we conducted vary in tone and style according to the particular background and personality of the individual filmmakers. There is also a complete diversity in the range of topics discussed, covering everything from mainstream and commercial to alternative and feminist. And they vary in thematic concern, depending on the artistic goals of each filmmaker. For instance, Penelope Spheeris is concerned with portraying violence as true to reality as possible in her work, believing it deters rather than desensitizes the viewer, while Martha Coolidge is concerned with incorporating a feminist sensibility into the traditional teen comedy genre. Euzhane Palcy is interested in telling stories that reflect a realistic vision of black culture and experiences that are specific to women and to black people. Amy Heckerling defines being typecast as a woman director, Lea Pool talks about feminist filmmaking in Quebec, Anne Wheeler discusses working within Canada's "Boy's Club", Randa Haines relays her feelings of responsibility as an image maker, Sandy Wilson talks about the use of personal experience as the inspiration for her storytelling, and Lizzie Borden focuses on the use of film as a political tool.

Since the majority of women interviewed are independent filmmakers or have come from a background of independent filmmaking, they can discuss the more personal/political side of filmmaking, and the struggles involved in getting their films realized.

The filmmakers included in this book also offer an intriguing look into the power and mechanics of image making. Among the subjects discussed are influences and inspirations, breaking into the business, choosing and preparing the screenplay, a woman's point of view, feminist cinema, sex and violence, censorship, women's on screen image, working with actors and crew, dealing with the money people, independent versus studio production, actress turned director, and advice to aspiring filmmakers.

One function of the book is to lay bare some of the complex factors which determine what eventually reaches the screen, and how women can and do make a difference in getting it there. It also attempts to define a feminist aesthetic and how it applies to women who work within the established industry, and those who prefer to undertake independent productions.

Twenty women filmmakers will undoubtedly reflect a wide range of viewpoints on any given topic. By putting their interviews together under one cover, the book will be a valuable resource, working in two ways. First, it will give the reader an opportunity to examine each artist individually. Second, it will also allow a chance to compare a number of different opinions in response to any given topic.

It is our intention that this book will stimulate new ideas about familiar films, as well as familiarizing the reader with an entire new body of work, some forgotten, some undiscovered, and all of it directed by women.

ONE

Karen Arthur

Filmography

Legacy (1975), Independent

Cagney & Lacey (1982-87), Episodic TV

Hart to Hart (1982), Episodic TV

Rich Man Poor Man (1976), ABC TV Mini-series

Mafu Cage a.k.a *My Sister, My Love* (1978), Independent

Charleston (1980), NBC TV Mini-series

Return to Eden (1982), TV Mini-series (Australia)

Victims for Victims (1984), TV Drama

The Rape of Richard Beck (1985), TV Drama

Crossings (1986), TV Mini-series

Lady Beware (1987), Scotti Brothers Entertainment

Bridge to Silence (1988), TV Drama

Evil in Clear River (1988), TV Drama

Bump in the Night (1991), TV Drama

Karen Arthur was the first woman to direct an American mini-series, *Rich Man Poor Man* (1976). Her emotionally charged television work includes episodes of *Cagney & Lacey,* and such movies of the week as the very powerful *Rape of Richard Beck* and the disturbing true life account, *Victims for Victims.* Born in Omaha, Nebraska, Arthur moved to Palm Beach, Florida when she was eight years old. Raised as an only child by her interior decorator single mother, she made her mind up early in life to be an artist. She enrolled in ballet, and by age fifteen was a featured soloist with Frank Hale's Palm Beach Ballet Company. A successful dancer, she moved to New York and added choreography, acting, and theater direction to her many talents. Deciding to explore film, she traveled west in 1971 and enrolled in a six-week crash course at UCLA. She took full advantage of her time there, writing, shooting, recording, directing, editing, and cutting the negative on her first fifteen minute film entitled *HERS.* From there she attended the first cycle of the Director's Workshop for Women at the American Film Institute. Arthur spent the next half dozen years raising the financing to make two independent features, *Legacy* ($70,000) and *The Mafu Cage* ($1,000,000). The former was invited to the Director's Fortnight in Cannes, and the latter starred Carol Kane and Lee Grant. Although both films were critically acclaimed, neither was successful at the box office.

The next feature film that she developed was *Lady Beware,* which took eight years to make. The film was difficult to finance because Arthur wanted to make a film about "psychological rape", but the major studios wanted her to portray the rape with physical violence. Eventually she got the film made at a smaller studio, but she didn't get final cut and the film turned out different than she had intended. Although her feature film work has been a constant struggle, television offers her an outlet to tackle tough social issues that interest her.

Q: *You've directed* Cagney & Lacey. *Could you tell me how the television series has been valuable to women directors?*

A: There are very few shows in television that will take a chance with young directors period, be they men or women. Barney, the producer of *Cagney & Lacey,* was always very supportive. He tried to bring fresh directing talent and women directing talent into *Cagney & Lacey.* Sharon Gless and Tyne Daly, the two stars of the series, were also very supportive of that.

I had actually applied to their program earlier and was unable to get involved because ORION said no, they weren't ready to use a woman director yet. I remember they looked at my film. They looked at *Mafu Cage* and the quote out of ORION was, "The films that women make are so female," as though that was a negative thing. But Barney fought and fought, and finally I got a chance. It was marvelous because we were dealing with issues that had to do with the heart, and the sensitivity of women, because of Tyne and Sharon. Yet it is a muscular show, an action show as well. So it allowed the directors, and the women who haven't had an abundance of opportunity, to work on action, to sink their teeth into that.

Obviously episodic television is the best place in the world to learn, because you do get to use the cranes and you do get to use all the Hollywood tools. *Cagney & Lacey* also deals with people whose sensitivity and sensibility is geared towards a woman in the work place, and as Tyne was, a woman in the home, and juggling those two situations.

Q: *Was it difficult trying to get a job directing when you first came out to Hollywood?*

A: I came out here to become an actress in film. Back East I had been a dancer, and a choreographer, and a theater director. I started directing theater out here and friends of mine said, "What are you doing directing theater? This is film town. You should make films." I didn't have a clue about film. As an actress, I thought after the film was done, why wasn't it out? I didn't realize there was an editorial process or anything. So I went to UCLA for a quick crash course and fell passionately in love with the process of making movies. I made my first little film and took it around thinking of course that the world would herald a new talent. I was patted on the head a lot by everybody. So I thought, fine, they need to see that I can really make a film. So I went out and made *Legacy*, which was a feature film. Then I dragged that around. It was 35mm, the whole thing. Again I was patted on the head. At that time women were not directing. There were no women directors. Ida Lupino was the last women to hold a DGA card. So I went to a friend of mine who was the creator of *Rich Man Poor Man* and it was just ready to go into episodic. And I begged him, I'd known him for many years, and I begged him to give me a chance. He saw my work, and he said fine, I will do it.

He went to the tower and he fought for me. They said, "four letter word her, don't give her the job." He said, "You don't understand, I don't want to fuck her, I want to give her a chance, she can direct." He put his job on the line. And that is how I got my DGA card. After that, when I would show up to work at Universal, the stage would be filled with crew from other sets who would wander in and out all day long to see the broad direct. They had the cigars and the whole number. But it was so wonderful for me to see that ultimately it doesn't matter if you're an orangutan. If you can direct, if the crew knows pretty soon that you can direct, then they let you be, and they're with you. It didn't matter that I had a skirt on, hypothetically, or what have you. I think today that it's very, very different. There have been enough huge successes, and enough huge failures by women to show that we're standing now shoulder to shoulder with our male counterparts. We're still not getting the quantity, but it's beginning.

Q: *What was the first day on the set of* Rich Man Poor Man *like for you?*

A: The first day that I arrived for work on *Rich Man Poor Man*, which was the first time that I'm dealing with 75 people now instead of 15, I walked in to meet with the A.D. [Assistant Director]. He said, "Well obviously we're doing this scene first, and therefore we're going to be down here in the living room, and you're going to want that wall out, I know you're going to want the camera here, so I had the guys move the wall so we're that much ahead of the game." And I stopped! I realized indeed that I did want the wall removed. I knew this was it, one of those moments where everybody's standing around watching to see how I'm going to deal with this. I said, "No, I think you should put the wall back." He said, "But you don't understand. I know you're a lady and it's the first time you're on a set, so you really don't know, it's going to take them half an hour at least to put the wall back." I said, "I think you better put the wall back." He said, "But then we'll be late doing this scene." I said, "Don't worry about it. We won't do that scene first. We'll do this scene first, because it's the same actors, it's the same wardrobe, and we're in the kitchen. So we'll just move to the kitchen while the guys are putting the wall back." Of course, at the very end of the day we finally got back around to shooting that scene. I said to him, "Now you can remove the wall. I'm the director, and you're the AD right?" He was a wonderful guy, very sweet, and actually he was trying to help me. But it was that kind of moment.

It reminds me of the Orson Welles story when the young filmmaker was directing a graveyard scene. It was Orson's first day on the set, and the filmmaker was down in the grave with the camera shooting up. Orson came and peered over. He looked down at the director and said, "You're not really going to do that shot, are you?" The young filmmaker looked up at Orson and he said, "Mr. Welles, if I do no other shot in this whole film I am going to do this shot." I think we all get that the first time out of the box, before we've earned a reputation that can establish that we know what we're doing. It's that old cliche, "I know you're a lady and you haven't been around that much, and I'm going to help you out."

Q: *Do you think that women get typecast?*

A: I think everybody gets typecast. The first film you make that gains recognition in any way shape or form, people will then say, "Why don't you do another one of those? This time paint it blue."

I've been fortunate to be typecast by making films that have to do with issues. Films that have to do with more serious types of statements, heavy dramatic statements dealing with psychosis or neurosis or what have you. That's great for me, because that's the kind of thing I want to see when I go to the theater. That's the kind of thing I want to read when I'm reading books. So I'm very happy to be typecast in that realm.

Q: *Do you think that films should be political?*

A: Oh, absolutely. No question about it. I don't think there's anything more powerful than being subliminally hit on all different kinds of levels, and film does that better than almost anything else. I don't think that everything should be that way. Obviously, in times of stress we need to relax. We need to be entertained. My hope is even within the films that I make having something to do with issues about women, I'm also entertaining people.

Q: *Tell me about your struggle to make* Lady Beware.

A: I took *Lady Beware* to Universal. We worked on it there first, and then it went into turn-around. After that I went to other studios and other financiers, but not much happened. I had an eight year history of going in and out of development, in and out of writers, in and out of turn-around, and I continued to drag this applecart around. Finally it got made. We made it in the summer, a year ago this summer, and it's just coming out now. I used to joke that all the people in Hollywood, all of the studios had gotten together and each studio had pitched in $20,000 so that finally I wouldn't pitch it to them anymore, and they wouldn't ever have to see me and *Lady Beware* again.

Q: *Why was there so much resistance to make the film?*

A: The problems were in the writing of it. It seemed to stem from the fact that I was opposed to physical violence. I was trying to tell a story about psychological rape, not about physical rape. My idea was to explore in this movie the myriad ways that women are taken advantage of, and fight back. It was not just to show a victim. I wanted to show the woman using her creativity and her imagination, the savvy she had as a human being to fight back and indeed to win. But everyone is more comfortable with physical violence. Potential investors would say, "Couldn't you just kill her cat," or "What if somebody who lives next to her is raped." The concept that somebody is dangerous even though they aren't physically dangerous at that moment in time was very difficult for people to understand. Ultimately, we had a great deal of difficulty getting the script made in the way I always wanted it to be made.

Q: *Do you think that women have a unique point of view?*

A: No question about it. From the first time that I read a book by a woman author, I started feeling things that I had never felt before. I asked myself, "Why am I feeling this?" It became extremely clear to me that it was because it had a woman's point of view. Even in film, in the early days, in the early 70s, because of the women's awareness groups and because of people trying to gain their identity creatively, women would come together in international film festivals and international symposiums from all over the world to share their work. There's no way you could sit down for a day and see twelve or fifteen films made by women and not realize that you're seeing something different. I think it's so important to mix these views. Even seeing women portray physical violence, it's different. There is a different sensibility. I think we have to nurture women's creativity and see their point of view, our point of view. And share with our male counterparts and see their point of view.

I know as we sit around in groups and discuss if there's a women's sensibility or if there isn't, that we're really divided. Many of us think that it's true. Many women don't feel that it's true. Then there are the films written by a women and directed by a man or vice versa, and you get a blend of sensibilities. There are also films made by women who obviously have a very strong male side to them, and you see that dominance as well as seeing their female side. Also, some men have very strong female sides and you see that.

Q: *Would you say that Penelope Spheeris' films are from a woman's point of view?*

A: Most definitely, most definitely. Penelope has been able to speak to us from a very urban, very raw place. Penelope to me is such a jarring filmmaker. Her films are very violent, disturbing, unsettling, and that's wonderful. She has that sense. But again, I can still feel the sensibility of this woman within all of that. I know that none of us want to be categorized into doing the sort of sob sister movie that used to be handed over to a female. We all want to be able to make *Apocalypse Now* or what have you as well.

Q: *Do you think you have different abilities as a female director than a man who is directing a picture?*

A: As a woman I can get certain things out of actors that if I were a man, I don't think I could. Sometimes the male ego balks with another male ego, or a male ego intimidates a female ego or vice versa. It's not saying one is better than the other, it's just saying that you can get something different.

As well, you're able to achieve something because of the same vibes. The vibes are different between a woman walking on a set and a man walking on a set. That was one of the reasons they went after me for *The Rape of Richard Beck*. They thought the film would be interesting coming from a woman's sensibility.

Q: *Why? What was that film about?*

A: *The Rape of Richard Beck* is a story about a policeman who is brutally raped, and how that changes his life, and his attitudes about sex crimes. The two producers, Henderson and Hersh, thought a woman handling a rape could bring to it a kind of vulnerability and understanding, as women have historically been the victims of this particular type of crime. Richard Crenna, who was awesome in the role, later said that he found he was able to be open and vulnerable in certain areas because I was there with him as opposed to what may have happened, although one never knows for sure, had it been a male presence. That may have presented a little bit more of an ego play or what have you. Our particular chemistry worked because of my understanding of the roots of rape and what he was trying to bring out as the victim in this situation. That perhaps allowed it to be more pungent.

Q: *And at the same time, it's a very tough film.*

A: Exactly. In that film you have a Seattle homicide cop who had always had a derogatory attitude towards the sex crimes division. His attitude was kind of like, that's rape and that's not terribly important guys. I'm in murder. He was always pulling rank when it came to which case was more important. If the person had raped and murdered, he wanted to take the collar for it because obviously the murder was the more important crime. He was also a cowboy who would go out at night and wander around Seattle. He would actually seek out and find people who were doing things, and he would rough them up when he was off duty. One night he got in a very hairy situation with a bunch of bikers, and they raped the shit out of him. He tried to cover it up, but there was a witness, and the witness let it out. Then when the whole precinct found out about it, he finally had to fess up. And at the same time of course he's going through the same symptoms which all of these women had been going through, which he used to say bullshit to. So it's a wonderful example of a reversed situation. It's a true story. The guy is now out, he's left homicide and joined the sex crimes division. He now teaches policemen throughout the country, lecturing on rape and attitudes about sex and sex crimes. So he's taken his experience and is giving it to other people.

Q: *Tell me about the American Film Institute and specifically the directing workshop for women.*

A: Living in California I was able to get involved with the AFI. First I had tried to secure an independent filmmakers grant. In fact I'd tried many times, about ten times I think. The last time I applied, I said you're going to have to give me a grant or give me a gold watch. They finally gave me the grant. I was also part of the intern program at the AFI which is a wonderful program. I interned with both Arthur Penn and Peter Hyams. This is all before the women's directors workshop started at the AFI. So when the idea for the women's directing workshop came up, of course I wanted to go. I had at that point made *Legacy* which was my first feature. I was really excited and wanted to try some other ideas. Coming together in that group allowed me the opportunity to experiment, to fail. I didn't have to be there addressing commercial cinema right away. It was the first group, the pioneer group. There was a lot of controversy over it because a lot of young

**Karen Arthur directing *Mafu Cage*,
with Lee Grant**

women filmmakers were dying to be a part of it and they could only take eight or ten of us. I forget now exactly how many were in that first batch. But there was a little annoyance that women of stature in other parts of the arts were being invited in. Lee Grant was in it. Margot Kidder, Anne Bancroft, and Susan Oliver, who was also an actress. Mia Angelou, who up to that point had been a writer. But between all of us, we sort of thought it was a wonderful idea, because there were documentarians like Susan Martin and Lynne Littman. There were first time feature directors like myself.

So as we began working, we began to see the value of working with these experienced women. Also from the AFI's point of view, they knew that these women had access to making films and were serious about it. These women would be able to go on and indeed make a dent in the industry. They would make enough of a splash that it would be like a beacon to other women, in later years, which indeed has happened. For example, Lynne did her film, and Bancroft did her film, and bit by bit little droplets began to accumulate in the water so that people in a financial position were able to say, it doesn't matter if it is a woman because ultimately it is that track record that allows everybody to relax.

Q: *Do you think that women executives have helped women directors?*

A: In the early days, there were very few women executives. They were there in sort of token positions. They really didn't have the clout to say yes to a film. They could say no to a film, but they couldn't really say yes. They could fight for us to a degree, but they really didn't have the power yet to say, "This is who's going to direct this movie and I stand behind this person one hundred percent." That has changed. Women executives now have an enormous amount of power that they didn't have before. How many of them are continuing to support and make things happen, I don't know. But I know that their position has changed, as our position is now changing.

Q: *Do you think that Hollywood is a boy's club?*

A: Most definitely. It's like any other craft. People have been around for a long time, and what they've been doing from the beginning, within the unions or whatever, is handing the jobs down — father son, father son, father son. And that still happens. Great producers would hand it down to their sons. Writers would hand it down to their sons. Directors to their sons, and there was a community that was built out of that. So women were editors. They struggled very hard to become writers, very hard to become producers, and now to become directors. But we still don't see it in the other crafts. I mean, how many women are in the IATSE in camera and in the other areas equally? When I'm making a film, if I'm producing or have raised the money for it, I always demand as many women as I can get behind the camera. But I try to balance it with men to make it harmonious. I don't think that films should be made by all women. I don't think that films should be made by all men. We live in a collective society. It's a wonderful energy when you're on a set and you've got half women and half men. There's a great sharing between everyone. There's a great sense of respecting each other. Gender goes out the window. It has to do with work, and the sensitivity of each person being seen and appreciated. I think that's healthy. I'd love to see more of that in Hollywood. This is the place of opportunity.

Q: *Have you had to make any personal sacrifices in order to work as a director?*

A: I don't know about making personal sacrifices. I chose when I was very young not to have children because I wanted to be an artist. I was more interested in having my children come out of my artistic work. So that was not a sacrifice. That was a choice that I never felt badly about. I'm myopic about my work. The magnificent thing about it is that it's so fulfilling, whatever the subject is. I worked on a mini-series about the Vietnamese boat children refugees. I didn't know a hell of a lot about that, and now I do. I'm able to speak with people who were in charge of the movement, of the refugee movement. People want to share information with you. So you meet kings, and scientists, and prostitutes, and junkies, and statesmen. The cornucopia of the world is there for you to learn when you're a filmmaker and you're serious about your research. That's such a gift. So I somehow never feel that I'm sacrificing, or that I've sacrificed. I love what I do so much that it's feeding me all the time. I don't feel a loss of anything.

Q: *What is your approach to directing?*

A: A film is made by a group of people. As a director, the most important thing I can do is to help inspire all of the creative people involved, to build an ambiance in which they can do their best work.

I try to inspire them towards their best, and encourage an atmosphere that we're doing this together, collectively, and sharing ideas. Obviously, the ideas eventually have to be filtered through the director. But that sort of collective vision is what goes on the film. It's that sense of family, and that sense of community. As a director, I think I'm there to be inspirational and to keep the candle lit for everybody.

Q: *How can an aspiring filmmaker get started?*

A: It's so important to realize that you don't start off being a director. You should start by learning a craft, and pay your dues. I was fortunate that I came out of directing theater and being a choreographer. I didn't know about film, so I had to learn about film. I worked in commercials for years as a script supervisor. Then I worked in documentaries cutting sound and negative and sweeping the floors of editing rooms or whatever just to be around celluloid, to learn what it was about. I never did anything really, really well. I did it as good as I could. But I was learning all the time, and putting the pieces together. At one point I thought, what I really need is more understanding about camera. So I went to Universal and I began to work in the loading room cleaning the slates and the clapper boards, and loading the magazines on the graveyard shift, from three o'clock in the morning until eight. I thought I would move into camera that way.

It's interesting, because so many of the women that I know who are now successful directors did the same thing. Randa Haines started out also doing script supervising, also being an editor. When I first met her she was an editor who had just made this wonderful film, and it was her first picture. People like Susan Martin and Jill Godmilow started by making documentaries or editing. There are so many women who learned to be a director or learned to be a producer by doing with their hands the actual craft. We do have the opportunity of non-union work within this country, even if you live in Nebraska. So do that before you finally make that ultimate commitment to go to California or New York or wherever you need to be to actually break down those studio doors and get in there.

TWO

Lizzie
Borden

Filmography

Born in Flames (1983), First Run Features

Working Girls (1986), Miramax Releasing

Love Crimes (1992), Sovereign Films

Inside Out (1992), Short within a Feature, Playboy Video

L izzie Borden earned a degree as an art major at Wellesley College (affiliated with Harvard University), before moving to New York where she painted and wrote reviews for *Art Forum* magazine. Deciding to switch from art to filmmaking after seeing a Jean-Luc Godard retrospective, she taught herself to make films by renting equipment and experimenting. Her first feature length, independent film, *Born in Flames,* took five years to make. A feminist, futuristic fantasy that takes place after a socialist revolution in the United States, *Born in Flames* is a powerful debut which brought Borden into the limelight. Besides gaining critical acclaim, the film racked up a number of prizes at North American and European film festivals. The film, which explored new ideas within the feminist movement, was also innovative in its approach.

Because of limited financing, Borden developed an aesthetic that lent an immediacy to the subject, by blending different film styles such as documentary, stock footage, and pseudo-documentary. Her innovative approach subsequently heightened the impact of the film. After struggling to make *Born in Flames* on a shoe-string budget, she raised a greater, but still modest amount of financing for her second independent feature, *Working Girls.* A film on prostitution, set primarily in a brothel, *Working Girls* attempted to demystify the role of the prostitute by showing the mundane routine of her work.

The film created yet another flurry of attention about the young filmmaker's talent, and played theatrically, grossing more that a million dollars. The success of *Working Girls* launched Borden's feature career. She left New York, setting her sights on Hollywood.

Her first studio picture, *Love Crimes* (1992), is a shocking take on female sexuality which stars Sean Young and Patrick Bergen. The film was short lived and less successful than her independent attempts in which she was calling her own shots. It will be interesting to see if Borden will stay within the Hollywood system or return to her independent roots to make her next film.

Q: *Your creative background is primarily set in the art world, so how did you get into filmmaking and why?*

A: I never intended to be a filmmaker. I started out as an art critic and as a painter, then I came to New York and got totally politicized by feminism. I discovered that painting was way too static, and being an art critic was too judgmental. It was before any kind of political art started being hot again. It was all abstract work and I had been trained as a formalist which was totally abstracted from any meaning that I could see within this culture. Then I saw a retrospective of Godard's films and I just freaked out. I was so jealous. I was looking at these movies and thought, "Why am I jealous? Why don't I do this?" So I did. I didn't want school to screw up filmmaking for me the way it had painting, so that's why I decided not to go to NYU. I taught myself everything. I rented cameras, tape recorders, and editing machines, and just did it.

Q: *What inspired you to make* Born in Flames *and* Working Girls?

A: Well, I guess I feel like an anthropologist. I like to go into marginal areas or dangerous areas where I have a lot of questions. For me the process of filmmaking is just a means of exploring those questions. When I made *Born in Flames* there was no script. I knew I couldn't write a script because if I did it would have been imposing an idea on something I knew nothing about. So the exploration in *Born in Flames* was about marginal women; it was about black women; it was about an underworld of women, a lot of gay women, and a lot of women that were very much on the barricades of the ghettoes in which they lived. For me it was an attempt to try to see what is the language of these women and how can I talk to them? So the framework of the film was a kind of microcosm for that interaction. With *Working Girls* it's really similar because the world of prostitution was closed to me. In doing a film I decided that I really had to present a lot of the questions that I had initially in approaching the subject matter. I don't know that I could do a film where I knew answers beforehand, and yet I'm not interested in doing documentaries because I don't like the arbitrariness of the documentary form where you just shoot randomly; where you have ideas and then the form; the subject, the content dictates the structure. Whereas what I like is elements of reality in which I can then decide to do what I want. Where I can really be the artist. I can be the dictator, in the way I want. In *Working Girls* it was like that. I wanted to present elements of reality in extreme close-up so people could see the rituals; they could see the realities of that world that was hidden. Yet a documentary would have only closed doors instead of open doors.

Q: *Do you use your filmmaking as a political tool?*

A: Oh, yes. For me film is a political exploration in itself. And for me, it is my only political exploration since I don't engage in any kind of politics outside. I'm not a member of women's groups, I don't go to rallies, I don't do any political work. But for me to choose a subject is always to ask political questions. A lot of people try to define me or my work as feminist-anarchist or whatever. I feel closest to anarchism even more than feminism, because I guess I'm really against any party line of feminism. And anarchism is a way just to say, "I'm calling that stuff into question," and in some ways the films that I do, I think they are political at the core in that sense.

Q: *When you made* Born in Flames *you had no background in filmmaking and it was a radical idea. How did you get financing?*

A: It was an impossible film to do. I mean I knew I couldn't get financing. How do you get financing? You don't have a script, and you say, "It's about all these black radical-lesbians who are taking over the media and then they're gonna blow-up the World Trade Center." Nobody in their right mind is going to give you money. I knew that so I financed it doing jobs as a film editor, and I'd work for a month and then I'd shoot one day and my money would be gone. I did that very additively — it's kind of like writing a very expensive novel.

But it was worth it. In a way, having a low budget from the beginning determines an aesthetic, and for me I wanted an aesthetic of cheapness for *Born in Flames*. With *Born in Flames* I started with practically no money. It cost something like $30,000 but so much of it was barter I don't know how much it would have cost had I paid people. I had to steal everything. Any time I needed a location I'd go and steal it. I'd steal the demonstrations. I would go to places like the airport and steal a scene and get out faster than the guards could stop me. And working with different camera people, I must have worked with twenty camera people, and when I couldn't find anybody I shot the film myself.

Q: *How did you finance* Working Girls?

A: I started out with $10,000 but it wasn't enough, so I decided that I had to make a studio in my own house. I couldn't even afford to rent an apartment because it would have been a fortune. We wouldn't have enough money for the rental and also the lighting units and all of that. It would have been too expensive. So I built a set at home, and I ended up doing a lot of the functions on the film too, simply because I couldn't afford to hire anyone.

Q: *Do you feel handicapped by financial limitations?*

A: I just think it's important to develop an aesthetic out of poverty in a way. Sort of the poverty of cinema, where you don't have any independent financing. For a lot of us who make our films based on grants, it's a whole different system than private investment. What happens is that when you finish a film like *Born in Flames*, you get rewarded. You go to festivals. You run all over the world. And then after that you get every grant in the book. But every grant in the book isn't enough to make a movie. You just think it is. So the important thing is to get the film in the can. And you don't even think beyond the can you just think, "Okay there's got to be a way you can edit this together." And that's kind of what happened with *Working Girls*. But basically, I think that the most elegant solutions are the simplest. That's why I like some of the other independent filmmakers around because they know what to do with very little money and they choose very elegant solutions for their problems. For example, Jim Jarmusch doing all his scenes in a master shot, or Spike Lee having his characters talk directly to the camera. For me, *Working Girls* was about one set, a very, very intense look at one place.

Lizzie Borden on the set of *Working Girls*

Q: *Why did you want to make* Working Girls?

A: I really felt that since so much about prostitution movies is so highly dramatized with psychopathic killers and heavy lighting, and weird angles and garishness, that I wanted to make a very simple film about work and allow the viewer to see it up close. To see the condoms and the rituals, and the towel room, and the hygiene, and the downtime, the boredom and the humor. So many films about prostitution — and most of them have been by men, but even the ones by women — tend to be highly sensational. The women in them tend to be highly victimized or there's a heavy sense of moralizing about the women. If they're not murdered by the killer, they're saved by the cop. That was definitely something I wanted to avoid in *Working Girls*. By creating a structure where you could see the entire day pass, I thought I could really focus on work and also show that the myth that prostitution for women is about sexuality *was* only a myth. By focussing on exactly what happens, how they deal with their sessions, the bedroom scenes, and even the comedic aspects or the horrible aspects of it, and by showing all of those things up close,

I could somehow objectify the work and have references to other kinds of work outside of the realm of prostitution. For me those things came together. Sometimes people ask me, well if you had two million dollars how would you have done the film differently? I don't really know.

At this point the aesthetics and the politics of the film, and the fact that it started out very low budget, were elements that I think informed my entire conception of how I was going to approach it.

Q: *Making a film is a tough enough task as it is. Do you find it even more difficult being a woman director?*

A: It's interesting because a lot of people have said, "Oh, as a woman, how can you direct, how can you be a dictator? How can you tell people what to do?" But I think women in particular, not all women, but I/we use more female approaches to directing. It may be more manipulative on some level, it may be more coercive, and it may be trying to talk people into doing things. And on some levels it's much more collaborative, I think. I don't feel like I go in as a dictator. I really like people giving suggestions and I take a lot of suggestions. For me I don't think that cuts down on who I am as a director. But my sense with directing is that you get to know what you want and even things you don't know that you can do, you end up doing. It's like those stories about a woman moving a car off her baby. You end up having the strength to do that and you grow into the role. I don't think that there's anything that makes a good director except being able to listen and being able to be open to suggestions. But that's how it works for me. That's how I feel I can be a better director.

Q: *Do you find there are any advantages to being a woman director?*

A: There's a point in independent filmmaking where being a woman is an asset because a lot of the granting agencies are very liberal. If you're a woman, or if you're black or Hispanic, you end up getting grants. So it's great for women in my position because we end up getting our projects funded. I think at this point in time it's an asset to be a woman in terms of the industry because everyone wants their token woman. But on some level that's also a debit, because not that many women can succeed within the industry. I know a lot of women who went to Hollywood after doing documentaries, and made one big film that wasn't a box office success, so they're not going to have another chance. Being a woman is a real liability in some ways because you're too scrutinized. You either have to do brilliantly or you're not going to be able to have a chance at all to do any continuous work. So my feeling is that being a woman helps and hinders based on whatever framework one is operating from. Also, it's impossible to make films from grants anymore. That's why I started on $10,000 and then we had to put together a limited partnership. It was very hard to get the money. I mean guys would come to see the film, investors, and they'd say, "Great, great idea but where's the killer? Why doesn't Dawn come in and kill the Madam at the end of the movie?" They wanted action and they wanted moral judgment. When I'd say, "No, that's not this film," they didn't give us any money.

It's hard because if you're a woman very often what you're trying to do is things that are more marginal and therefore you're censored by whatever economic systems occur in this culture that say, "No that's not an economically viable idea." But as it turns out if you make a film that does well people say, "Oh, anything you want to do next." It's kind of what's happening with *Working Girls*. We couldn't get any money after the grants, and now since it's doing well people are calling me and saying, "Hey, what's your next project?" So it's kind of ironic that it's only box office that ends up making things easier, because that's economic censorship at its worst. I'd almost rather deal with the censorship of a censor board or a ratings board because at least there you know that the ideas can be confronted. You get arguments, you get dialogue about it. There's often an outcry and the outcry ends up politicizing a lot of people. However, with economic censorship no one's politicized in the process, you just end up not being able to make your movies.

Q: *Do you feel you have a women's point of view in your films?*

A: That's an impossible question. I don't think that there's a women's vision in directing a film, or a male vision, necessarily. There are a lot of feminist men making films and a lot of women who are totally identified with men as they're making their own films. Although I admire some of her work, someone like Penelope Spheeris is very much identified with young teenage boys.

So my sense is that it's an approach. Not content necessarily, not anything you can judge from the aesthetic. It's an overall approach that some women have or some men have that can qualify them as feminist directors. The only thing I feel about a feminist approach to filmmaking is just that we as women have to make our own images about whatever we see. That's what surprises me about people looking at *Working Girls* and *Born in Flames* and they say, "But you're a feminist, how could you do this movie?" My feeling about prostitution is about making a film about prostitutes where it shows them controlling prostitution and therefore shows me as a female director controlling the images that I want to be seen about prostitution. I think that's the most we can do as women. By putting out our own images, and choosing how we want to show these images, we are in fact changing the world. I think images work on a much deeper level with people than any kind of argument. Even in a porno film or an erotic film, as women I think we have desires. We have images that turn us on. For a long time pornography has been dominated by men, and by the images that turn them on. So I don't think as women we have to say pornography is bad, we just have to put out the images that are hot for us. And of course everybody will scream and carry on and say, "Oh that's not fun for me." Every woman will have a different idea. But the more that we can do that in terms of a visual notion the better, and even contradictory ones where, within a feminist framework, women are presenting different points-of-view. That expands the notion of feminism beyond any level of dogma.

In terms of pornography as well, there's got to be a sense in which we don't have artificial distinctions between eroticism and pornography. Because what happens is that it's so personal and so individual, that if we do away with straight up the snatch shots, if that's not what turns us on, and end up substituting hot images for us, even very dreamlike images that come from our own experiences, then I have the feeling that we'll be turning ourselves on. And if we're turning men on too that's fine. They can be turned on, as long as we are also able to enjoy some of the stuff that we've been denied enjoying for so many years.

THREE

Martha Coolidge

Filmography

More Than a School (1973), Documentary Short

Old Fashioned Woman (1974), Documentary Short

David: Off and On (1975), Documentary Short

Not a Pretty Picture (1976), Documentary Feature

City Girl (1983), Independent

Valley Girl (1983), Atlantic Releasing

The Joy of Sex (1984), Paramount Pictures

Twilight Zone (1984-85), Episodic TV

Sledge Hammer! (1985), TV Pilot

Roughhouse (1985), TV Pilot

Real Genius (1985), Tri-Star Pictures

Plain Clothes (1988), Paramount Pictures

Rambling Rose (1991), Midnight Sun Pictures

Lost In Yonkers (1993), Columbia Pictures

Martha Coolidge was born in 1947 and grew up in a suburban environment close to New Haven, Connecticut, then entered film at the age of eighteen. She has recorded sound, shot camera, worked on commercials in New York and a television series in Canada, studied acting, and directed live theater. Coolidge helped to start the Association of Independent Video and Film in New York during the 1970s, and produced and directed the short documentaries *Old Fashioned Woman*, about her grandmother, and *David: Off And On*, about her addict brother. In 1976, she made her first feature length film, *Not a Pretty Picture*, a dramatized re-creation of Coolidge's own rape. The success of that film prompted her move to Hollywood. After five years of working on projects that never went into production, she was finally offered a screenplay. Producers Wayne Crawford and Andrew Lane wanted to have a woman's sensibility reflected in their movie *Valley Girl*. Bringing Coolidge on board gave them what they were looking for — and more.

From her background in hard hitting social documentaries, she brought a feminist perspective and sense of integrity to the teen comedy genre. The film launched the career of then unknown actor Nicholas Cage, and it spun the phrases "awesome," "bitchin'" and "for sure" out of the Valley and into the mainstream. *Valley Girl* secured her the opportunity to direct her first studio picture, *The Joy of Sex*, for Paramount. Finding herself typecast in the teen genre, her next success came with the ten million dollar special effects hit *Real Genius*, this time propelling Val Kilmer into the limelight (who later played Jim Morrison in *The Doors*). While directing teen comedies, Coolidge continued to search for material that would depict her vision of the world, discovering the screenplay for *Rambling Rose* in a dead script pile. The film took five years to finance. A tender coming of age picture set in the South, *Rambling Rose* features real life mother and daughter, Diane Ladd and Laura Dern, who both received 1992 Academy Award nominations for their performances.

Most recently Coolidge has bravely come forward in the mainstream media proclaiming charges of sexual harassment that are prevalent in Hollywood.

Q: *What was it about* Rambling Rose *that first attracted you?*

A: The first thing would be the incredible language, and the very specific characters. But the themes of the story in the end of course are what touched me deeply. I've found that my movies are always about people struggling with significant choices. And that's really what this story is about. It's about learning to love, and forgive, and not to judge, and not to feel superior to and different from another person.

Q: *You had the project for five years before it was shot. What finally made it happen?*

A: I gave it to Laura Dern when I first read it, and she wanted to do it, and about a year later I gave it to Diane Ladd. I had also been giving it to financiers. And Edgar Shark who'd had it seventeen years had tried to set it up with me, and with many other directors, but it was always rejected. I think the material really frightened people. So Laura and I made a list of people to approach to be the Executive Producer. As we started running through the list, she started dating Renny Harlan and asked me if Renny could read it. I said sure. He started reading one night and couldn't put it down. He said, "I have to do it."

Laura said that I was directing it, and so he said that he'd produce. Renny took it to Mario Cassar and, like a dog after a bone, would not drop the subject until Mario made it. And Mario loves the movie. This is the same man who made *Rambo* and *Total Recall* and was Executive Producer of *Basic Instincts* and *Die Hard Two*. But they made the picture, and they did it supportively, and it was a great experience. They're a great company to work for.

Q: *What was it like collaborating with a mother and daughter team, Diane Ladd and Laura Dern?*

A: They don't work the same way at all. It was like working with any two unrelated actresses. They both have very different styles of working. It's obvious that they love and respect each other a lot though, because we'd finish a scene and each one of them would come up to me privately and ask, "Wasn't she great?"

Q: *How did you feel when your direction earned each of them an Oscar nomination?*

A: They were terrific in the roles, and I think also that the female characters were unique. So, between the acting and the characters, I think that's what does it. Because I think Bobby and Lucus were equally as good as Diane and Laura, but it's not so unusual to see great male characters.

There are many more interesting and different roles for male characters than there are for female characters.

Q: *How do you create a comfortable working atmosphere for the actors?*

A: First of all I listen. I like a quiet, friendly set, as opposed to a bunch of screamers. And I often try to take the actors suggestions into consideration. I respect that they have a very hard job. So I make a lot of my decisions based on what the actors have to do. If Laura has to cry all the way through a scene, and she finds it difficult to cry, then I try not to do too many takes and I try to use multiple cameras. So she's not stuck crying all day. Or if Bobby Duvall tells me the take in a scene is going to be take number one, then I move in to shoot his close up first.

Q: *How did you begin making films?*

A: Well, I started as a singer actually. I was a folksinger first of all and loved it, loved performing. I was a very shy kid and then the singing kind of got me into musicals and acting. I sort of evolved from singing into acting and was doing both in high school. Then I finally directed my first play in high school. I was suddenly able to step back off the stage and see the whole picture, and be able to use my knowledge and use my ability to see the whole show. I said, "This is it, this is what I'm meant to do."

Then I went to college and made my first film. When I made that film, something I had tried to avoid because all of my friends were dropping out of college to become filmmakers, I'd thought, "God, who would want to do this? It's too competitive, I don't want to compete with all these people." But then I made my first film and said, "My God this is what I was meant to be."

Q: *How did you end up in Hollywood?*

A: I'd been making films in New York for about ten years and finally felt I'd tapped out my growth potential in that market place. Budgets were getting bigger and bigger. I was raising all the money for the films, putting the partnerships together, and it just became too much. I also wanted to get back into working with actors and dramatic film. So I felt the only place to go was Hollywood. I knew enough to know that it wasn't a town to go to without having something to do. So I applied to the AFI for an AFI Academy internship, and they selected me as one of their candidates. Then I had to be interviewed. I was very lucky that an internship came up right away and I interviewed with Robert Weiss, and he asked me to be his intern. I found there was a lot of interest in me as a woman director from the agents. And, after all, I did have ten years of filmmaking under my belt and a lot of films to show.

They were documentaries and that made it a little bit difficult to make the transition into dramatic film. I was just releasing *Not a Pretty Picture* at that time. I had a lot of projects come and go.

I developed two scripts in New York that I brought with me, so I had some scripts that I owned. But one starred two women, and that was way ahead of its time. Nobody wanted to do a film with two women. And the other one was a very serious picture about someone going insane, which didn't appeal to the Hollywood eye either. After a year and a half or so here, I decided to make a little partnership and without money took some friends and made a film called *Bimbo*. It was a little comedy, all men, written by a man. I wanted to show that I could do comedy and male material. So that was a little show piece I had, and it ended up being the only film that I made in that period of four and a half years that I was in Hollywood before *Valley Girl*.

Q: *What else were you doing in that period, besides* Bimbo *and* Valley Girl?

A: I started doing a very long project with Francis Coppola. It was a rock 'n' roll, musical love story which was called *Photoplay*. We started from scratch. We started researching it. Now as I told you, I started as a singer but I hadn't listened to music in ten years. When I first put the band X on my record player I thought "Oh my God! Am I ever gonna really learn to love this music?" I mean, Devo sounded like noise. And within several months I was having a complete rock and roll experience. My life was charged with rock 'n' roll.

It was two and a half years of working every day, putting this project together, going through several drafts of the script, hiring cameramen, and postponing the start date, going through all of this, until finally Francis canceled the picture. That was very heartbreaking. At that time I'd had several other possible projects fall apart in Los Angeles and felt that it was really time to call it a day here. The whole period was one of the most traumatic, wildest experiences of my life.

Q: *After you left Hollywood, what prompted you to return?*

A: I came back in a very circuitous manner. I came back to Los Angeles via a film I shot in Toronto. It was called *The City Girl* and it had shut down before it was done. It had run out of money. So I went to New York to try to get someone to buy the picture. Finally a friend of mine, Colleen Camp, said, "Oh, why don't you come out to Los Angeles. I'll set up some things for you, maybe you'll meet Pete Bogdanovich." I brought the little reel I had back out to Los Angeles, feeling very skeptical. I showed the reel to Peter and he said, "I love this film. I love it. I'll buy it." He actually pulled it off. He got some young lawyers on it and they bought the film and we finished shooting it. When that film was in a rough cut, I showed it to some friends of mine, one of whom was Andy Lane.

Andy had written a script called *Valley Girl* with his friend Wayne Crawford. He gave me the script to read. I realized that it was the first time I'd ever been offered a "go" picture in Los Angeles after four frustrating years there and a year-and-a-half or so away. So I took the script home and prayed I would love it, which I did.

Q: *What did you like about* Valley Girl *when you read the script?*

A: *Valley Girl* is your *Romeo and Juliet* story about a young Valley girl who has very superficial values. She's into her clothes. She's into her friends. She's into status symbols. Her boyfriend is also like that, but she's bored with him. Then she meets a boy from Hollywood who is a punk. He's purporting to have very strong ideals about how to live life and how superficial Valley people are. And of course, they fall in love and the friends don't approve. It's a kind of *Romeo and Juliet* story, which is based on the actual split between Hollywood and the Valley. It is a little bit exaggerated.

Q: *Do you think that film should be used as a political tool?*

A: Well I've never felt that I was a propagandist in my filmmaking or primarily a political filmmaker. Even when I was making documentaries, I was not an information documentary filmmaker. What I've always been, I feel, is a storyteller about people.

So my documentaries tended to be about people, their stories, very subjective. And my features also tend to be that way. What I've always felt is that I am a feminist. I was formed during a period when the feminist movement was very strong, when women really emerged, when we learned a great deal about our society and about men and women. I came up through a very political time, through the sixties. I'm a very consciously ethical, moral person. In fact, I would say that I am a moralist. I'm very American. Those are the things which I cannot make a film without. I can't lose those things. In becoming commercial, I've never lost those qualities. I can't do movies that promote values which I feel are misogynistic, or anti-humanistic, or promote irresponsible political or social attitudes. I do however, and always did, even in documentaries, have characters in my movies who may be misogynistic, immoral, or unethical. Because I think these are the things in life that we're all dealing with. In *Real Genius* you'll have a Dr. Hathoway who's the representative of a very corrupt sell-out type of person in our society. All of these elements are elements in life. So they are elements in drama.

Q: *What kind of material have you been offered since the success of* Valley Girl?

A: Unfortunately, *Valley Girl* is perceived as being a teen comedy. Now *Valley Girl* is actually a pretty serious movie.

It's very funny, but it has quite a serious love story, and it has serious conflict in it. And I treat the characters with respect. The material that I've been offered in the wake of *Valley Girl* in general so far is inferior to what *Valley Girl* was. It is stupid. And sometimes the girls all are called pigs, or they're all prostitutes, or they're all exploited. Ethnic people are treated with great disrespect and abusiveness. I mean, it's incredible what goes on in the genre of teen comedy. And what's amazing is sometimes I'm shocked. I get a script and I read it and I think, "How could they possibly offer this to me? What is my public image that they would think I would ever do this?"

Q: *Is it a problem finding good material that you want to direct?*

A: To me it's not a problem, because I simply turn it down. What does become a problem is typecasting. And I think that's something that everyone deals with in Hollywood — the directors, the actors, everybody. It's a problem. You are generally given a certain type of material and that's all. That's ridiculous. For example, I kept hearing the same story, "Women can't do action." So then I was offered the *Sledgehammer* pilot. I was offered it because it was comedy. But nobody said, it was teen. Because you see, it was adult comedy, it's about adults. It also had guns and action and stunts and all this in it. So I said, "Okay, this will be fun." It was a comedy but since it had guns, at least they couldn't say that I haven't done guns.

So I did *Sledgehammer*. And suddenly that changed my image in television from, "She can only do comedy," to "She can do action." I also did three serious *Twilight Zones*. So I've done a lot of special effects now, and I've been offered a lot of pilots. It's amazing how your image suddenly changes. In the movies though, I'm still getting generally teen material and silly comedies.

Q: *Why are women generally typecast into directing teen comedies?*

A: Well, what's interesting is that where a lot of us got our breakthrough was in comedy or teen comedy. And then we're facing the problem of breaking out of comedy or teen comedy. And what's crazy to me is, here I am a filmmaker with a very serious backlog of pictures made on very serious subjects. But in Hollywood, I had a meeting today and they said, "How curious that a woman who made *Valley Girl* and *Real Genius* would be interested in making our picture, which is a very serious film." And I said, "That's not so curious if you know my early work."

Q: *Has the success of* Valley Girl *made it easier for you as a film-maker?*

A: I think *Valley Girl* certainly made a big change in my life in the sense that it opened an enormous number of doors that had not been opened before.

It was a commercial film and suddenly I was an acceptable director and I was on a lot of lists that I hadn't been on before. I think that every success that has happened to a woman director has changed things for other women directors. I mean, I have experienced the effect of *Valley Girl* on me. It was my film, so it was a big effect. But I know right around that time is when suddenly other women were starting to get jobs. I think that *Valley Girl* had something to do with it, as did *Fast Times at Ridgemount High*. That film made a lot of money, and opened doors, and made things more accessible for other women directors. *Desparately Seeking Susan* was very important too, because of its acceptance by the public. It was a highly respected film. All these films have done women a lot of good. The sad part is that the flops made by women are somehow held against all woman directors. More so I think than similar flops by male directors.

Q: *How has the situation changed for women working in film today since you started out twenty years ago?*

A: Well, the situation with women directors is obviously changing very quickly. The door was opened and it's not going to shut again. That's great. It has its ups and downs because every time there's a success it seems to open a little wider and I think if there were a bad failure or a series of failures it would probably close the door a little bit, but it doesn't mean it's ever going to close again. There are more and more experienced women.

I think one of the biggest problems in the beginning was that it was a chicken and an egg. People said, "There aren't enough experienced women to hire and at the same time, we want to hire

Martha Coolidge on set

them but how do they get experience?" So it was really a problem. Now there's more and more experienced women and so that isn't really so much the problem. It has more to do with breaking into certain areas like action, real big pictures, the real big actors, "A" pictures.

Q: *How about women in power? Has that changed?*

A: When I first got here, which was ten or eleven years ago, there were very few women executives. And the woman executives in the business in general, now this is a generalization, were not in positions of great power, and their jobs did depend on the opinions of the males around them. There was not a great networking or support system between women. Generally if you were a woman, you didn't want to hang your . . . In fact when I first got here the advice I got was not to hang my career on another woman, because she'd be having a hard enough time, she's not going to give you a break. It generally seemed to be true, although there were a few women here then that were networking with their friends. But they'd generally been in town for a long time and knew each other. So that has changed. I think women have now advanced in their positions. There is a lot more authority in their respective jobs. We can all do things that help women more openly, and take risks. It's much different. I can't even describe to you what it was like when I first got here. What it was like when I started in the business was unbelievable. I mean I went for my first jobs and said, "I really want to be a director." And they said, "Don't tell anybody you want to be a director! My God, just tell them you're dying to be a production assistant. You really want to be a film editor some day maybe. And whatever you do, get a manicure, wear eyelashes, and more make-up."

Q: *Do you think women filmmakers have accomplished a lot in the last twenty years?*

A: It's been very hit or miss. Elaine May's features came out at a time when I was just starting to make films. I thought she was brilliant. I really admired her. She was very important to me in terms of an American Hollywood ideal. I'd seen Agnes Varda's films, but that didn't mean that it applied to the United States. So that was very important. But then after Elaine, there wasn't anybody. There was this sort of gap. Then there were the Joans — Joan Silver, Joan Tewkesbury, Joan Darling — and they were great. They were really paving the way, and they all got their shots, and Claudia [Weill], too, at that time. Each of them are good successful working directors. But those films didn't do well, or they weren't marketed right, or something. Nothing happened right enough with them to make Hollywood say, "My God, women are it. This is it. We've got to make more women's pictures."

So there was a little rush of those four films, and then it was a kind of dead period again when everybody backed off. Suddenly there were closed doors again. Then they sort of opened again. So it has been very hit or miss.

Q: *How important is box office? Is it the main factor considered when people want you to direct a picture?*

A: Well, it's funny. There are certain mysteries, the mysteries of Hollywood, which are only answered once you've been here for a little while. Now one of those mysteries is box office. When I lived in New York and Toronto, I wondered, "What is it? Why do

Martha Coolidge

they make these films? Why don't they make these other films? Why don't they make the movies I'd like to see? Movies my friends would like to see?" Then once you come here and you start seeing the ebbs and flows of Hollywood thinking, you start to understand a little bit more about how the audience is measured, which is really what box office is all about. The general mentality is to get a big hit, of course, and to make a film which appeals to everyone. But you see, who is everyone? Everyone is the man, because, and I've heard this many times, "It's the man who buys the ticket. It's the man who decides what movie they're going to see, not the woman. Men go to movies by themselves." Okay, you could argue the point that some women go to the movies with each other, but basically it's couples and the guy decides what movie they're going to see. So a lot of movies are made with a very male leaning. And of course, the people who are making the choices and decisions about these movies getting made are men at the studios. And look at the track records. They haven't been wrong. They've had lots of hits. But I still feel there are movies that could be made and could be hits that would not necessarily be the hits that would appeal to just that audience.

Q: *Do you find that being a woman creates additional obstacles than the usual ones present in the film industry?*

A: It's a very difficult thing to talk about, because it's a very difficult thing for the person herself to be able to measure. I think that there is no question in my mind that, first of all, had I been a man I would have come out to Los Angeles right after completing film school. But I didn't because I was a woman, and there were no women working in Hollywood at that time. So I stayed in New York and I made films for eight or nine more years. I made a lot of films. I think that when I came out here there was interest, but it was kind of like the new buzz was, "Hey women directors," but nobody was hiring them. There was a lot of interest, a lot of action, a lot of meetings. In that period of time, I learned that certain people would meet with you and like you. And frankly the people that wouldn't work with you wouldn't meet you. It was that simple. So it's very hard to measure if there is discrimination and what the attitude is towards women. Frankly, they're not going to invite you in to a meeting, and they're not going to give you a project if they don't want to work with you. Where we make progress is when they're saying, "Let's look for who's going to direct this picture," and on that list are three guys and three women.

That's it. Indiscriminate of whether you're a man or a woman, but having to do with the material and whether that person is going to bring something to that material. And that is something that still has a long way to go from where we are now.

Q: *What is the difference between working as an independent film-maker and working for a studio?*

A: Most people think that the biggest difference between an independent film and a studio picture is the size of the crew, and the responsibility toward the crew, and the intimidation of working with a large crew. The truth is that an independent film and a studio film are organized in very much the same way. The biggest difference between the two is in fact what's over your head. Usually in an independent picture you're the producer. You raise the money. You're not dealing with anybody. The pressure from above is much, much less than in the studio feature or the big budget feature. The more money, the more people above you, the more pressure, and the more the director becomes squeezed between the frying pan and the fire. On one hand the authority on the set, on the other the person who's working for all these other people and somehow has to satisfy all their needs. It becomes a much more diplomatic job, dealing with two forces.

Q: *Do you believe there is a distinct women's point of view that is different from a man's?*

A: I think that there is something uniquely inherent in being a woman in terms of a perspective, but I don't feel that all women are similar in their perspectives on the world. I think that being a woman brings each woman something unique in her perception, where if she were a man she wouldn't have the same perception of the world. But I don't think that you can completely generalize. The more women directors that we have, the more we will see the differences between women, and to me that is what's so exciting about having a lot of women directors. After all, that's what's exciting about having male directors. Look at Howard Hawks,

Sam Peckinpah, and Ingmar Bergman. Those are three very different people. And when we can see women who are that differentiated and that different working in the world, it will be a very exciting time.

Q: *Do you think that female directors are changing the on-screen image of women?*

A: I think that the image of women on screen is changing, and it is changing partially because of women directors. No question about it. I will not present a woman or a girl in the same way as a man doing the same picture. I think that *Real Genius* is a very clear example. I don't think I present men in the same way. I think that's very important too. I think women see men in a different way.

But certainly women's roles and women as bimbos are not going to be a common image in women's pictures. But still there will be women who will present that. After all, there are women in this society that believe their entire purpose is to be attractive to men. They're going to make pictures too. But I think that it will continue to change, that we will see more interesting female characters.

Q: *What are the qualities of a good director?*

A: I think what makes a good director is a person who has a very strong point of view about life. The most important role of the director is point of view, and an attitude toward the material. You have to present that point of view and attitude on the screen. Secondly, they should love actors and be very good with people. And thirdly, I think you have to enjoy what is essentially a collaborative art. You can be a leader, but also be a person who's open to ideas and input from a lot of different areas. If you are a total authoritarian type, you will be nothing but unhappy directing.

Q: Not a Pretty Picture *is a disturbing film. How did it come about?*

A: *Not a Pretty Picture* is an autobiographical film. There is cutting back and forth between a fictionalized depiction of the events in my life leading up to my own rape in high school, and the events following that rape, and documentary footage of the rehearsals of the rape scene within the making of that picture. People have called it Brechtian and I think that is probably the closest to dramatic relationship that the film has. I shot the rape scene in *Not a Pretty Picture* in a rehearsal format because I did not want to have another movie where the audience is forced to participate in a rape scene by watching it as an exciting action sequence. I wanted to do a rape scene which somehow revealed what rape is, and yet not get you too excited and want to see it completed. I wanted to always distance the audience and keep them separated from participating in that rape to some degree. I think that the rehearsal and the actors, intercutting between the rehearsal and talking about how they felt, what that rape scene did to them ended up accomplishing that in a very unique way.

Q: *Do you have any advice for aspiring filmmakers?*

A: Perseverance is the most important thing, and the ability to recognize opportunities when they come along, because they don't come by very often.

FOUR

Julie Dash

Filmography

Working Models of Success (1973), Short

Four Women (1975), Short

Diary of an African Nun (1977), Short

Illusions (1983), Short

Praise House (1991), Short

Daughters of the Dust (1992), American Playhouse

D *aughters of the Dust* claims breakthrough status as the first dramatic film made by an African American woman to receive major theatrical distribution. The filmmaker responsible for *Daughters* is forty-one-year-old Julie Dash. She had the idea for the film in 1975, but it took seventeen years before her stunning feature film made its debut to the resounding praises of audiences world wide. Born in New York City and raised in the Queensbridge projects of Long Island City, Dash was introduced to filmmaking in an after-school workshop at the Studio Museum of Harlem in 1969. But at that point she wasn't dreaming about being a filmmaker because images of African Americans, especially women, had never suggested to her that they could do things like make films. Dash persevered, however, continuing her interest in film production by attending City College in New York. When she graduated several years later, she decided to pursue filmmaking as a career. Relocating to Los Angeles, she attended a course at the AFI where she made *Four Women*, an award-winning experimental dance film. In 1983 she released *Illusions*, her first dramatic piece and most critically acclaimed work to date. Set in 1942, *Illusions* is about a black movie executive passing for white in the wartime Hollywood film industry. Like much of Dash's work, it tells stories on many levels, playing on themes of sexual, cultural, and racial domination. With the success of *Illusions*, Dash was ready to begin intensive research on *Daughters of the Dust*.

She began by collecting stories from her relatives, then she searched the National Archives in Washington, the Library of Congress, the Smithsonian Institute, Harlem's Schomburg Center for Research in Black Culture, and the Penn Center on St. Helena Island just off the South Carolina coast. Dash emerged with an original script that tells the story of a Gullah family preparing to leave the Sea Islands and journey to the mainland at the turn of the century. She then spent years raising the money to make it, carrying out other duties on the film at the same time. When *Daughters* was released, Dash was rewarded for her tenacious struggle. There was tremendous response to the film on the festival circuit and during the film's theatrical release.

Q: *How did you get into filmmaking and why?*

A: I started a very, very long time ago. I started in 1969 in a film workshop when I was in high school. It was a place to go to be with my friends and play around with the equipment. Looking at the equipment was very confusing, but mastering it was exciting. I knew nothing about filmmaking, the history of films, or film theory. All of that came much later. The after-school workshop drew me to film. It was a workshop provided by the local government after the Harlem riots in 1966. They pumped a lot of money into Harlem and into black communities to create after school programs for students to keep them off the streets. And luckily I was able to fall into one of those after-school programs. But nothing drew me to film. It just happened. It was slow in coming. It didn't have anything to do with making dramatic films. It was just some place to go. Like people go to pottery workshops, or after school arts and crafts. And filmmaking workshops for me were like arts and crafts.

Q: *What is* Daughters of the Dust *about?*

A: It's about going away from home with the possibility of never returning, because in those days with a journey that far away the likelihood of you returning was remote. It's also about not abandoning your culture. It's about abandoning your home, but not your culture.

Q: Daughters of the Dust *was a stunning directorial debut. How were you able to put the money together for it?*

A: I had to do a trailer first, a ten minute promotional trailer to get the money to do it. And the success of my previous films helped too. I'm always telling people that you don't have to do a feature film. It doesn't mean you're any less of a filmmaker if you work in shorts. I've been doing shorts for many, many years. And because of the success of those films I was able to get financing to do a feature-length film.

Q: *How were you able to make such a gorgeous period piece that looks like it cost a fortune with the modest budget you had to work with?*

A: For one thing, everyone was working under their normal scale rate. It was like a labor of love. In fact it was a labor of love. Everyone felt moved by the story and by the region that we were working in, which was the Sea Islands of the south. It's a region where African captives were first dropped off in the United States before they were sold into slavery. Everyone wanted to see this film made. They were doing more than their share by wearing two or three hats, doing their own jobs and helping with others. We all were, black and white, the whole crew. And that's how it got made. I'm glad it looks beautiful. I'm glad it's done. It was a horrendous experience. It was a grueling experience.

Q: *What inspired you to make it?*

A: A lot of things. I wanted to do something on the Gullah, or the Geechee people and their history because it's very important to African Americans. The Sea Islands is an area where the African captives were first dropped off after the middle passage. It's also an area that many scholars are flocking to today, to study a retention pattern. They're studying the retention of our cultural morays, our religious beliefs. They're looking at just how retention manifests itself over hundreds and hundreds of years. You can really see that in the Sea Islands. It's an area that's still very, very West African in its look, in its customs and in the way the people speak.

Q: *Everything looks so lush in the film. You break the stereotype of impoverished blacks, showing the Peasant's as a family of total prosperity. Was that your intention?*

A: It's a prosperity of a sort. They were prosperous because they lived on what they could reap from the sea and from the earth. They still eat like that. My relatives ate like that. It doesn't mean that they were wealthy. It was just that you didn't see them toiling in the land, in the soil, which you so often see. You always see black folks depicted in those situations. In the film I would show the family having a Sunday gathering, they would have a family day. They'd bring all the food they had together and they'd lay it out in a very sumptuous way and have a grand feast. That seemed to disturb a lot of people. It's like we're supposed to be hovering over, or crouched over, one single bowl of mush all the time. Well that was not the case. It's from a whole different perspective. I wasn't around at the turn of the century, but that's the way I remember it. That's the way it was in all of the research. It's from my point of view as an African American woman as opposed to white males who are usually directing these type of films. We see their imagination, their fantasy of what it would look like, their production design, their Eurocentric view on how it would look and feel, and their art directors and so on and so forth down the line. That's why we see a history on the screen that's a history of someone's whim or fantasy.

I've been to some Question & Answer sessions after the film is screened and white males have stood up and told me that my film was totally inaccurate. It's mainly because they've never seen a film like that before. Everything that we did, every meal that we prepared, every dress that was sewn, everything was based upon actual photographs from the archives of the Penn Cultural Center on St. Helena Island. And in fact we didn't even go as far as we could have because we didn't have the money. I couldn't do the hats that they wore. They wore these very interesting hats.

Q: *The film is very poetic to look at. Could you talk about how you approached the unique visual aspect of the film?*

A: I wanted to do a very impressionistic film, because the film is basically about memory and recollection. I wanted most of the major scenes to start off as tableau, using wide screen masters rather than a lot of close-ups. I think that when you remember things, you remember them in tableau. We also used a lot of slow motion and step-frame printing in various sequences for the same reason, because it also gives a memory or déjà vu feeling.

Q: *Why did you choose the voice of the unborn baby as the narrative?*

A: Contrary to what I had been taught formally about there being only one narrative voice, I realized as I was writing this particular story that there were two. There are always two points

Promotional still of Julie Dash for
Daughters of the Dust

of view in any situation, and often many more. But I wanted two points of view. I wanted the point of view of a child who was part of the family but was not born yet, and the point of view of a great-great-grandmother who had seen them come and was going to see them go. I liked that play of opposites, the ancient and the future play of opposites. Here you have this child that's not born, but she's a part of the family. She's running around intermingling with the children and trying to affect their future, or her future. She's trying to get things straight so that when she's born everything will be cool and calm and going along smoothly. Then you have a great-grandmother who's giving her point of view for way, way beyond. So you have the past, you have right now, and you have what will be.

Q: *Do you believe that films should be political or a political tool for change?*

A: I think all film is political whether you set out to make it political or not. I think *Mary Poppins* is political. Anything on that screen that depicts a certain class, or whether the people have or do not have points of view — it's always making a political statement. Whether it's parody, fantasy, straight dramatic narrative, whatever, you're making a statement about culture, class and all of that. You're making a point about how you see it. Your point of view, whether you're going to parody it, or make a comedy of it, or whatever, it's all political. People who say they're just doing something for entertainment, I think they're very misinformed about the power of film.

Q: *Do you want your films to reflect a woman's cinema or an Afro-American cinema?*

A: Both. I think that's one of the reasons why my films are so disturbing. So foreign if you will. They're so alien because, number one, they're focusing on African American women and speaking to African American women, and, number two, they're from the culture of women. I always try to set my stories within the culture of women and I think that that's very disturbing visually, viscerally and emotionally to white males. And the reason I keep saying white males is because they're generally in the position of privilege when they are watching films, or producing films, whatever. You know that generally the story is from their point of view and it's for them.

So even films about women, that have nothing to do with African American women, will disturb them to no end. So then when you have a film that's about women, and also about African American women, it's like too much. They disengage from it for the most part. Not all men, but largely men do that. And they ask, "Well what is this about?" They say that it's about nothing, and they become very hostile. It's not just that they don't like it, it actually makes them hostile. I think that happens because they're not privileged by it, and they're operating from a position of privilege everywhere else in the world.

Q: *What qualities do you think make a good director?*

A: You have to have something to say, and say it with a lot of passion. Always be aware of the power of film. Don't go into it naively, talking about it like it's just entertainment. That's hard to take anytime I hear people say that. So know the power of film, know that you're dealing with a hypnotic medium. I think that with each film you should try to change the world in some small way. And I think you should try to change it for the better.

Q: *Have you overcome obstacles, or made any personal sacrifices in your career?*

A: There's a book on the production of *Daughters of the Dust* and I talk about an obstacle in that. I was pregnant in the pre-production of *Daughters*, and I had to have an abortion. We were on location, scouting locations in pre-production. I was pregnant and I had to make a decision. And I really don't think that it's all that unusual. That kind of decision will have to be made by a lot of women directors or career women. If it had been a different type of task that I had to perform, it could have been possible to do, but filmmaking is like construction work, it requires your physical as well as mental ability. And because I have a daughter, I also knew that I get very sick during pregnancy and I was already starting to get sick and fatigued. I didn't tell anyone about it. I just flew up to Atlanta, had it done and came back. That was a tough decision, but it was either that or delay the film.

Q: *What advice do you have for aspiring filmmakers?*

A: I think they should know that as a woman everyone will tell you, for the most part, that your work is not commercial, that it's uninteresting, and chaotic. If you're working from a woman's point of view, you're going to run into massive problems. Be prepared for it, let it roll off your back, and just go ahead and do what you want to do. Everyone seems to want you to make the film that they wish they could make if they had the strength or the creative juices. Everyone.

Once you get into production, or even when you're doing the writing, they question, "Why don't you do this? Why don't you do that?" But I say, "Why don't you make that film?" Because you have to make the film that you want to make. You have to shoot the film that you want, because when you get into the editing room, you can't just whoosh it up. When you're trying to do something very different, you have the most opposition. Then afterwards, everyone just loves you to death. All along, with each film that I've made, including *Daughters of the Dust*, which was my eleventh film, people have been telling me that I'm crazy, that it wouldn't work. Those same people were grinning in my face. And the same thing is happening now. Since *Daughters* I've written some new screenplays and I get the same response, "It will never work. There's no other film like the one that you're proposing. It's not commercial. Why don't you do something else?"

Q: *I imagine after the success of* Daughters of the Dust *you had Hollywood banging down your door.*

A: Not really. Everyone wanted to take me to lunch because they secretly loved the movie, but they couldn't tell their superiors that. It's so strange. They tell me they loved it, but they're afraid that I can't do a straight narrative. I ask them to look at my other work. Then they say, "Yeah, but it wasn't a feature."

There's always something there. There's always an obstacle they throw at you. My life is not determined by people in Hollywood, by what their dreams and desires are, because they're just treading water themselves. It's musical chairs out here.

Q: *Has anyone been inspirational or instrumental to your career?*

A: So many different people. I guess for the most part the black women novelists of the early seventies. They're the ones. Alice Walker, Toni Morrison, Toni Cade Bambara. They're the ones because when I started reading their novels in college, I thought, "Why don't I ever see films like this?" And it made me want to see these films. I was already making documentary films at the time, and I said to myself, "Well, I'm a filmmaker, hmm....Why don't I do films like this? How do I learn how to do this?" So that's when I came to Los Angeles, to attend UCLA and learn how to make dramatic films.

Q: *In what way did these voices inspire your direction?*

A: I was stunned when I started reading their work. I thought, "Why hasn't anyone ever told me about them before?" I was just completely stunned because these were the people that I recognized so well. I recognized people in my own family in these novels.

I'd never seen that on television before and certainly not in the theater or cinema. And I felt cheated in a big, big way. So I started thinking, "Well, forget all this making films like newsreels and such, I'm going to make the films that I've always wanted to see. I'm going to start making those films."

FIVE

Jill
Godmilow

Filmography

Antonia: Portrait of a Woman (1974), (co-dir.) Documentary

The Popovich Brothers of South Chicago (1978), Short

Nevelson In Process (1979), (co-dir. with Susan Fanshel) Short

The Odyssey Tapes (1980), (co-dir. with Susan Fanshel) Short

The Vigil (1980), Short

At Nienadawka with Grotowski (1981), Short

Far from Poland (1984), Documentary

Waiting for the Moon (1987), Skouras Pictures

J ill Godmilow, a pioneer in the independent documentary movement on the East Coast, entered the film industry in the late 1960s as a film editor in New York. Godmilow's 1974 feature length documentary _Antonia,_ about symphony conductor Antonia Brico, was made with folk singer Judy Collins and nominated for an Academy Award. She was also instrumental in half a dozen portrait documentaries that were made during this period, all of them on people who pursued creative vision with strength and courage.

In the early 1980s, Godmilow undertook her second feature length project _Far from Poland,_ a film that would blend fiction and non-fiction footage and would include the filmmaker as a central character. Although different in style from her other documentaries, it is similar in its message, in that it gives dignity to people who are not afraid to go against the mainstream. It has been heralded for breaking new ground in documentary film language.

The melding of fact and fiction in _Far from Poland_ led directly to her next undertaking _Waiting for the Moon,_ a film based on the lives of Gertrude Stein and Alice B. Toklas. Since little about their personal lives is well documented, Godmilow and screenwriter Mark Magill constructed "possible portraits" of the two women. They became intrigued with the idea of reconstructing history as acknowledged fiction. Wanting to workshop some of the scenes, they submitted their first draft to Robert Redford's Sundance Institute, and were accepted to develop the screenplay further. It was there that American Playhouse offered to commit partial funding, which prompted producer Sandra Schulberg to find the rest of the money. Godmilow's directorial debut was well received, picking up glowing reviews for Linda Hunt's performance as Toklas and Linda Bassett's as Stein.

Godmilow continues to develop films from her New York loft, which is both her home and work base.

Q : *Is it harder if you are a woman to break into and then continue working in the film industry?*

A: I'm asked that question all the time. Is it hard being a woman filmmaker? Yes, it is. But the problems have to do with being raised in this culture. Feeling legitimate giving orders. Feeling legitimate believing in your bizarre way of doing it up against the critical expertise and talent of people who have done it twenty-five times more than you, and who say you can't do it that way. Those are the problems of being a woman filmmaker. Feeling entitled, feeling legitimate, trusting yourself, asking for what you want. I struggled with them all the way through. There are other problems, but that's the big one. The sense of legitimacy. And that you get from the culture, not from the film industry.

Q: *What is the best way for young women to enter into the film industry?*

A: The classic route for women in the film business, I think, has been through the editing room. There are a lot of reasons for that. It's interesting to speculate, but I think for the most part it was a way to get the intelligence and the ability of women into the movies, but through a role that was essentially non-threatening for the director. In fact, I think a woman editor is less threatening than a male editor. Women know how to make a suggestion and put an idea up there without saying, "Me, this is my idea." Instead they say, "Why don't we try this," or, "You always wanted to do something like this, why don't you try that cut there." We know how to do that. We're raised in a culture that teaches us how to do that. We learn it from our mothers. We learn it from our teachers. We learn it from our peers. So in some ways, it's the natural place for a woman to go in the business, and we are very good at it. Fortunately, it's also a good place to learn how to be a director.

If somebody comes to me and says, "How do I get to be a film director?" I say, "Get into the editing room." Because it's there that you are able to learn, and to see how film is a construction. And that is essentially the most important thing to understand. You can learn about acting, and you can learn about writing, but if you don't understand how bits and pieces of sound and picture end up making something that has movement and rhythm and flow, you don't know anything. It doesn't matter how well you can direct if you don't understand how the pieces will fit together in the cutting room. In fact, I think it's the ideal place to learn how to be a director. So women are fortunate for once in that sense. We're extraordinarily fortunate. I think also that women will keep being major film editors. They already are in almost every country. It's rare to see a French film and not see a female editor. And it's actually not uncommon in American films either.

Q: *Are there any women directors who have been inspirational to you or whose work you particularly admire?*

A: I saw a film a couple of years ago by a German director named Helga Sanders that blew me away. Every now and again you see a film that you just wished you'd made, because if you'd made it, you'd stop right there. It's that good. Helga's film did that to me. It was called *The Trouble with Love*. It didn't get distributed in this country, but I think it's the best women's film I've ever seen. It's the most intelligent. It's truly a woman's vision, and it's totally entertaining at the same time.

I like the work of Chantel Ackerman very much. She's a Belgian filmmaker, and I think she's always interesting. I think her film *Jeanne Dielman* is a great breakthrough film, not just in women's cinema, but in all cinema. I think Yvonne Rainer is an important theorist in film. She is a difficult filmmaker to comprehend, but she's always pushing for the new space, the next problem that can be tackled, and really opening it up.

Q: *Are there any women directors that you feel have opened up doors for other women?*

A: I think a woman that makes any type of film paves the way. I was thinking about who inspires me, who opens up film language for me.

Now, even getting a film made is so hard, as you know. I was once a rash, young woman, but I'm no longer so rash, so critical. I respect almost every film that gets made just for having been made. And for women, not so much because the industry's against them, but for women to take on that burden as products of a patriarchal society, I respect every one of them. Every woman who makes a film in some way creates road for the next person to go on.

Q: *Do you believe women are ghettoized in documentary filmmaking?*

A: I don't think that women are ghettoized in documentary any more than men are. The same thing could be said about men that is said about women. In the last five years, most of the men who are now making features came out of documentaries. To me, documentary was a way of feeling legitimate making a film. In other words, the "right-onness," the attachment to a social cause. For me, those things legitimized my projects. I don't think, even if it had been possible ten years ago when I was becoming kind of hot as a documentary filmmaker, I don't think I wanted to conceive of dramatic story. Somehow being righteous. It comes out of the sixties. Being on the right side, creating a cinema that put into the world the voices that spoke about the issues that mainstream cinema wasn't talking about — that was what one wanted to do.

Q: *Why did you start making dramatic films?*

A: A frustration at having arrived at the end of documentary. I felt that very strongly in my last non-fiction film, which was a film called *Far from Poland*. It expresses that frustration directly, and actually tries to deconstruct the whole documentary form. As I made it, I realized that it was my farewell song to documentary. It was just that the game of reality that's basic to documentary, to non-fiction cinema, was a game that I felt I could no longer play. In fact, about a third of it was done with the use of dramatized scenes. The film is about solidarity with women strikers in Poland. The shooting depended entirely on a visa to get in to Poland, and I couldn't get into the country. It was an interesting documentary problem. I had the money. I had the contacts. I was interested. I was even there when the strike started, but I couldn't shoot the footage. So I decided to speak about Poland instead. After thinking about it, I said, "What is this trick? What is this footage of Lech Walesa in front of the Polish parliament that legitimizes me to speak about Poland?" It's no more the truth, no more reality than dressing up an actor like Lech Walesa and writing the script for him.

So I think intellectually, filmmakers like myself, documentary filmmakers, were becoming quite frustrated with certain conceits about documentary. I think that propelled them into writing, into taking responsibility for the films they were making. There's a way in which documentary filmmakers, myself included, don't take responsibility for what's said in the film. They allow people to speak for them. And then, under the guise of only creating the truth, by only using what they found when they shot, don't acknowledge authorship. Don't acknowledge that they are writing a text in the cutting room, in the choice of who speaks. I was frustrated also with the conceit of that. I wanted to make a film that said, "This is what I wrote, and this is what I meant to say."

Q: *How were you chosen to attend the Sundance Film Institute?*

A: Well, it's one of the nicest stories in film history. Actually, I think we had enormous luck. It was the right moment, the right time, and the right connections. Mark and I wrote three or four scenes from the idea we had which was the beginning of *Waiting for the Moon*. We sent them around, but there was no interest. Nowhere. We applied for grants, and got turned down because it was at a moment when the funding agencies that normally fund films were not involved in dramatic full-length feature films, no matter how cheap they were going to be in the making.

So we inadvertently applied to Sundance. One day we got a call saying that we had made it through the first five rounds, and when was that first draft going to arrive. We had nothing written. So I said, "You better just throw out our application. We can't possibly make the deadline. It's three weeks away." They said, "Can you make it here in four?" I turned to Mark, and he said, "Yes." So we left the city, went up to this place we knew, and in four weeks wrote a script. It was accepted at Sundance.

Q: *What are the qualities of a good director?*

A: About half way through the shoot of *Waiting for the Moon*, I came to believe that charm is the most important thing. A director is a manager type. I'm talking about the shooting experience now, which I find most gruelling, the most scary. You're on this schedule that's not to be believed. You're going to shoot three scenes a day. I had a five week schedule which is twenty-five days of shooting. You're essentially managing a lot of high-powered, experienced — sometimes more experienced than you — talent. All of which, whether it's the lighting department or the actors, want more than there is. And the director ends up being a sort of focus in the struggle for another half an hour to put up a nice light in the back of some set, versus another take. Or another twenty minutes for the actress to rehearse on the set before we start to shoot. So charm, of which I think I lack enormously, would have saved the day many, many times. That's really a big requirement.

I found that there's very little active creativity on the part of the director during the shooting. I think the writing, casting, putting together of the thing, conceptualizing of it — the choices that you make in pre-production going into the shoot are the serious ones. Once you're shooting, it's like a capitalist production in the world. You take a million dollars worth of talent, materials, energy, and experience, and in six weeks or five weeks, pour it into a little 35 millimeter strip of plastic . It's a management job for the most part, and only rarely highly creative. Only rarely is there a situation where you go, "I got it, I got it."

For the most part you are driven to produce shot after shot after shot. You work on these tiny bits of film and trust that this script you have, this model of it all, will hold up when all those little pieces have to go together. That's what makes a good director. Passion at that point, forget it. The passion is what you need to get to that point. After that it's endurance. Some sort of knowledge that you'll get through it, that you'll live, and that it will all cut together.

Q: *Do you feel that there's a feminist phobia in the film industry?*

A: I think that the industry's about making money. It was actually weird to discover that this thing I'd been calling the film business all my life, was in fact actually a business. Once I was making a film on the level that *Waiting for the Moon* was made, a million dollar film, I discovered that was true. You see, women's

Jill Godmilow on the set of *Waiting for the Moon*, with Linda Hunt

cinema is still marginal, or cinema that has a decidedly feminist point of view, or that treats the subject of women in a way that's not voyeuristic. Those films don't make as much money. I think that's the essence of its feminist phobia. I don't think that it's ideological. I think it's financial.

Q: *Do you feel that women filmmakers have a responsibility to their audience when creating female characters on screen?*

A: It's hard for me to prescribe what women filmmakers should do. In the end, the only prescription you can make is for yourself. To me, the most important thing to do in cinema right now is to attempt in some way to constitute a cinema that changes the image of women in the world. Women have been used in cinema as an object of desire, as sisters, as mothers, as lovers. They are always projected on the screen for both men and women to desire. I mean, I desire Katherine Hepburn as well as a male audience desiring Katherine Hepburn. Can you create a cinema where that is not the sole existence of women in cinema? I tried to do that in *Waiting for the Moon*.

Q: *That type of image reconstruction. Is it much more difficult for Hollywood filmmakers than it is for independent filmmakers?*

A: I think that's a major reason why getting to make a film using Hollywood money as opposed to money you raise by yourself is extraordinarily difficult for women. It's primarily difficult for women who see changing women's on-screen image as their task, because that's against the entire mainstream of Hollywood. Cinema is essentially illusionist, escapist. A dream-like experience, where you come from your home, you pay your six bucks, you sit down in the dark, and you release yourself from the trials, tribulations, concerns, and the limits of your own life. You enter a fantasy time and space in which there are beautiful women and exciting lives.

Can you make a cinema that's not about escapism? Can you make a cinema that's not about focusing the audience on wanting to be who they're not? Can you make a cinema where your audience is essentially alert, observant, fully integrated with all of their capacities, with their rational mind, with their integrated abilities? Can you make a cinema with all of this active, and still make good cinema? That's pretty much what women filmmakers are taking on right now. With few exceptions, most male filmmakers are not taking it on right now. I think it's why women filmmakers are the most exciting filmmakers in the world. To do that, you've got to change some of the language. You can't work with the old mythic filmmaking techniques. You've got to break rules. That's why women's cinema is so interesting. It's breaking all the rules. That's a very exciting thing to be a part of. So for women who feel that way about the task of cinema, it's a pretty exciting time.

Q: *Which other women filmmakers are taking that task on?*

A: I think Lizzie Borden does it, both in *Born in Flames* and *Working Girls*. She tries to construct a cinema that has the classic puritan object in it. A prostitute. The subject of hundreds of millions of films. And she tries to keep us interested in a film about prostitutes where the main point is to see how mundane the life of a prostitute is.

The Marxist equation is, it's work, just like any other work. It has a rhythm. It has it's own boredom. It has its own repetition, and it's done to incur income. *Working Girls* is done to totally deglamorize prostitution. That's a radical film to make. *Born in Flames* as well, to the degree that it simply postulated a future, without being futuristic. Without fantasy it insisted that a time will come, whether it's a socialist revolution or whatever — a time which will speak about women's rights and equality, and five years after that, there will be no such thing. She positions you without fantasy, and engages you in what that will mean, and what kind of action you can take at that moment. That's radical cinema.

Q: *What is your definition of a political film?*

A: I've come to feel that film is political not because it prescribes the "right-on" political attitude, but because it changes the language. The truly political film is the film that changes language. Films that create a language that has been impossible, unspeakable previously. That makes it possible to think things that were unthinkable before. That's political filmmaking. So that the most political film in the world, or what looks like the most political film in the world, is not always political in that sense. *Platoon,* in fact, would be analyzed as being not a very political film, or the *Killing Fields* for that matter. It looks like a political film, but to me it takes the genocide of Cambodia and makes it a backdrop for a male love story. I don't call that political filmmaking.

So, in the higher sense, in the more intellectual sense, I think that film is political, but only when it's used by a political person. And I think that's rare. Those films are usually more difficult. They make audiences uncomfortable. So they're not prioritized by the culture. They exist, and they grow, and they have their audience, but I don't know if they'll ever be mainstream films. That's why I think it will probably be two hundred years before women's cinema dominates the culture, or before what I call a truly feminist film is a blockbuster hit. An audience comes to the movies for something else, not politics. Basically they still come for entertainment and escapism. There is an audience that comes to the cinema for something else, just like there are people who come to the bookstore for something other than escape. But that's pretty much a marginal audience. So far, women's films have been addressing that marginal audience.

Q: *What experiences have you had with your films around censorship?*

A: The first press release that the distributor wrote about *Waiting for the Moon*, which is a film about two lesbians, Gertrude Stein and Alice B. Toklas, talked about them as companions. I had to say to them, "Look. Let's not do that. It's going to embarrass me to deny their lesbian relationship." There's that kind of censorship. There's the censorship that wants to describe a film as generally as possible, and as innocuously as possible, because their lesbianism might turn off a section of the audience. Or they don't want the film to be thought of as a lesbian film.

That's a level of censorship, and it's the only level I've ever run into. The fact is, when the objection was made, the text was changed. So I can't say that I've been censored. But there's always that force in the culture, that will try to create product as suitable for the largest possible audience. Now the largest possible audience in this culture, in this country, means the one that nothing offends. If lesbianism offends, then it must not be described as such.

Q: *Do you censor your own material?*

A: I'm not the censoring type. I don't think I'm ever going to be in a position of feeling I had to, or should forbid any sort of cinema to be made or exhibited. But, I'm sort of a prude in my own tastes. I don't like exploitation of people in any form. Certainly not in pornography, or what we think of as pornography, or as exploitation. I don't like it when it's lesbians, and I don't like it when it's heterosexuals. It's not that I see something wrong with it. It's just that I don't like the idea of an audience being invited by the cinema to be in a bedroom behind closed doors, watching how two people relate to each other sexually. It's one of the reasons there isn't a sex scene in *Waiting for the Moon*. Essentially, by what right do I have to say, "Come on into the bedroom and watch how Gertrude and Alice touch each other," or how they kiss. I'm not comfortable with sex scenes in cinema. Not anybody's. But again, I don't think that I would censor others. I just don't want to see that. I want to meet people in cinema as I meet them in life.

I don't want a false intimacy that allows me to be a fly on the wall watching them. I also don't like scenes where people are having nervous breakdowns in cinema. I always feel, "Why am I allowed to peek at that?" I'm not interested in a cinema that does that. I don't call it censorship. It's an aesthetic choice. It has to do with what kind of relationship I want between what I'm showing and what the audience sees. I want an audience that knows it's watching a movie. I don't want a pretend audience that pretends it's not there as it peeks and watches. One basis of cinema is that. It is voyeurism. It's being able to look and see something that you can't normally look at or see. Being invited through the back door to peek. I'm probably trying to make cinema without using that, because I'm not comfortable with it. I can be pulled into it, pulled in as a voyeur, but I don't like the idea. I especially don't like the idea at this point, particularly with lesbian sex. I wouldn't offer it to a general audience because women touching each other has been at the center of male pornography for years. Therefore, I don't think you can offer that in cinema without it giving men a chance to have all sorts of fantasies. So, that's it. I don't feel comfortable saying, "Oh look at this."

Q: *Did* Waiting for the Moon *make a big difference in your career, for example, make the next projects easier to finance?*

A: Well, I think that it did make it easier in that I'm not a first time director of dramatic features, but beyond that, the timing has turned out bad. In terms of producing what I would call the marginal, non-commercial feature film, it hasn't helped a great deal. I think it would be a little harder if I was going out there for the first time, but it's been a terrible economic time.

SIX

Lee
Grant

Filmography

The Stronger (1976), AFI, Short

The Wilmar 8 (1979), Documentary

Tell Me a Riddle (1981), Filmway Pictures

A Matter of Sex (1983), NBC TV

When Women Kill (1983), HBO, Documentary

Nobody's Child (1984), CBS TV

What Sex Am I? (1985), Documentary

Down and Out in America (1985), HBO, Documentary

No Place Like Home (1988), CBS TV

Staying Together (1989), Hemdale Pictures

Battered (1989), Documentary

L ee Grant was born Lyova Haskell Rosenthal in New York City on October 31, 1927. A respected actress with two Emmys and an Oscar among her many awards and nominations, she made her stage debut at the age of four in L'Oracolo at the Metropolitan Opera. At eleven, she was studying with the American Ballet, and her teen years were spent studying acting and establishing herself as a Broadway talent. Grant made her screen debut in the film version of *Detective Story* in 1951, recreating the role of the shoplifter that she had made popular on the stage. That performance earned her a citation for Best Actress at the Cannes Film Festival and her first of several Academy Award nominations.

On the heels of that success came the era of Hollywood blacklisting. Grant, who was married to blacklisted screenwriter Arnold Manoff, was exiled for twelve years and was unable to work. Her long, impressive list of film roles since her return to the screen in 1966 include *Shampoo*, which earned her an Oscar, *In the Heat of the Night*, *Voyage of the Damned*, *Plaza Suite*, *Nylon Ceiling*, and *Peyton Place*.

In 1975, Grant turned her interest towards directing and attended the American Film Institute's directing workshop for women. While there, she made a short film from an Isaac Strindberg story, *The Stronger*. It brought her critical acclaim. Since her move behind the camera, Grant has directed a long string of successful documentaries beginning in 1979 with *The Willmar 8*, an hour long film that documents the lengthy strike held by female employees at a bank in Willmar, Minnesota. She later directed a dramatization of that film for television, entitled *A Matter of Sex*, which starred her daughter Dinah Manoff.

Her dramatic debut as a feature film director came in 1981 with the film adaptation of Tillie Olsen's novella, *Tell Me a Riddle*. Her acclaimed television movie *Nobody's Child*, a startling portrait of a woman's lifetime spent locked in an institution, starred Marlo Thomas, and earned Grant a Director's Guild Award. In 1986, she was presented with her second Oscar, this time for directing her documentary *Down and Out in America*, a film about farmers, hunger, and poverty.

Grant presently lives in New York City with her husband, producer Joseph Feury. They jointly own a production company that produces feature films, documentaries, and TV movies.

Q: *You had a successful career as an actress. Why did you decide to become a director?*

A: I decided to become a director because I was not obsessed as an actor anymore. I was not as motivated. Being an actor is very hard, especially if you have a tremendously perfectionist background, where being an actor is not enough. You have to be a great actor. You know that every time you go out to work it's got to be a new experience, a new exploration. And I have stage fright. I have always been a person with stage fright. Not so much in front of the camera as on stage, which was where I started. But there was always an element of it so that first days, for instance, are very, very hard for me. That whole wondering ... will I cross that line through the looking glass and be the character, and will it eventually come together? So that acting for me is not always an easy thing. It's a hard thing. If I'm not motivated, if I'm not driven to find parts that I've never done, and to put myself on the line, then it's hard for me to find a reason to act. And after the Oscar, which was ten years ago that I got for *Shampoo*, a lot of my motivation left. And it wasn't because I got the Oscar. It was because I had somehow associated Hollywood with the people who kept me from working when I was blacklisted.

What I'd realized in getting the Oscar, in that flash on the stage, in getting it, was that the enemy was in my mind. It was not really there. The people who had been involved in blacklisting me, and all the other people whom I knew who were either dead or not working anymore, had been gone years ago. That had been a symbol in my mind, to get back to a place where everybody had been thrown out. But it wasn't real. I was fighting dragons, and there was nothing to fight anymore. And so my own kind of restlessness, and the fact that I have a very low threshold of boredom, started to take over. The acting wasn't enough. I mean, the things that you always got that you thought that you wanted just weren't enough.

Q: *How did you start directing from there, how did that happen?*

A: Little by little I started to look for things that would involve me totally all the time. I went to the American Film Institute and that started the ball rolling because it took away the mystique that these people on the other side of the camera know some mysterious quotient that those of us in front of the camera can never know.

Q: *Has acting been helpful to your career as a director?*

A: Acting is a tremendous foundation for everything, especially directing. First of all, as an actor, you have to break down the script, you have to break down your objectives, you have to break down your beats. You have to see your character in conflict with the other characters since all plays and all theater are built on conflict. If you've been trained properly, you're trained to know a script. As well, you have to leave yourself open for the whole emotional life and the whole emotional journey that you're going to take. You're trained to push certain buttons in yourself, to know that certain emotional memories are going to bring up other things. So that in knowing yourself, you get to know what will trigger emotional things in other people.

Q: *You were in the women's directing workshop at the AFI. What was that like?*

A: It was the first women's workshop at the AFI and everyone was kind of thrown together. Nancy Walker was in it, Lynne Littman, and Karen Arthur. We were all told to pick a subject, any play we felt like doing. While they were all talking, I was just looking around the building we were in. It was this extraordinary mansion. I was just looking at the place and thinking, what could I do that could use this place because it's very kind of 18th century. And I got the idea of using *The Stronger*. I'd always had ideas about it that I'd never seen done, and it gave me an opportunity to do them. So that was it. They gave us a little bit of money to do two little pieces and I threw all that money into one.

We did a black and white tape of it. It was really interesting, and so they gave me a scholarship to do it properly.

Q: *How did your first feature* Tell Me a Riddle *come about?*

A: I was doing *When Are You Coming Back Red Rider* in El Paso, Texas. The book *Tell Me a Riddle* arrived and a letter from these three young women who said, "We saw *The Stronger* and we thought we'd get in touch with you and see if you'd be interested in directing this." And I read the novella that night and it was like a miracle. It was so beautiful and so important, and opened up my head and my thinking in places I just hadn't gone in so long. I wrote them back saying that I would do it under any conditions, at any time. That I would wait as long as they needed. That this was something I really wanted to do. And it did take a long time. They had to go to their cousins, their aunts, their dry cleaners, and try and raise two dollars, three dollars, twenty dollars. And it took them six or seven years to raise the money. It was an incredible job they did.

Q: *What is* Tell Me a Riddle *about?*

A: God. How do I describe *Tell Me a Riddle*? *Tell Me a Riddle* is a classic. It's a novella by Tillie Olsen. It is the story of two Russian immigrant people who were married and who were at a point in their relationship where they had nothing to do with each other anymore. That's where the film starts. And she becomes very ill. He sells the house without her knowing it. And it's their trip together to visit their children that makes them learn to know each other again.

Q: *How do you prepare for the actual shooting of your films?*

A: First of all, I always have rehearsals before making a film. I know that as a new director — I've only been directing for seven years — so I know that I need that time, so that it won't be taken on the set. Every kink is worked out before. With rehearsals, the acting problems are erased. If they weren't solved there, they were there in the backs of the actors minds to be solved. For instance, with *Tell Me a Riddle*, I had two geniuses. I had Lila Kedrova and Melvin Douglas and I had a wonderful cast, Brooke Adams and the rest of the people. So that the actual making of the film was just one wonderful experience after another.

Q: *After your first film,* Tell Me a Riddle, *what happened to your career from there?*

A: Nothing. First of all, it was distributed by a bankrupt company. Film Ways was the only one who took it and they went bankrupt. And of course the whole secret to making a wonderful film is to find a wonderful distributor. One who will publicize it and distribute it properly, and get it to the audience that it needs to get to. *Tell Me a Riddle* didn't really hit its audience until the Z channel in California put it on. Then suddenly I got calls from people that I hadn't heard from in years. Jerry Hillman had a party at his house, and Michael York and a lot of people sent a letter they'd signed, saying this is the most important picture we've seen and we want you to know that. And this was about two years ago. So it really disappeared until cable took it up. And when people saw it on cable, it was a tremendous kind of discovering. But its life as a feature film was just nipped in the bud.

Q: *How does your production company operate?*

A: My husband, Joe Feury, and I have a kitchen company. If we're not doing dramas, we're trying to get documentaries done. We don't stop making films. I think we made four films last year. One was an after-school special, one was a documentary, and one was a movie of the week. We just never stop. The principle behind our company is work. That work begets work. And that is the same thing as when I was an actress. I'd see people in Malibu at the beach getting that same blue in their eyes as in the ocean, that kind of washed-out thing that you get from too much hash or too much booze which is what happens when you're waiting, waiting. You have so much time in your life.

I've always had a terrible sense of time moving. I've always had it even as a child. As a matter of fact, the only two lines in poetry that made any sense to me, that hit me, were, "I have fears that I may cease to be before my pen has gleaned my teeming brain." I had that sense of yes, I feel that too, and I was twelve. That I may cease to be before everything in my brain is out. So I'm involved in a process, not in the success or failure. I'm involved in the doing of it, so when something happens, like an award comes in, it's a tremendous surprise.

Q: *Can you talk a bit about your marriage to Arnold Manoff, and the effect of the blacklisting period in Hollywood?*

A: My first husband, Dinah's father, gave me a great education in politics. When I met Arnie Manoff, who is also a fine writer, he was in the early contingent of blacklisted writers who were named with the Hollywood Ten, that whole group of writers who left Hollywood and came to New York. I was eighteen and a half or nineteen when I met him, and I'd never read a newspaper. I didn't have any idea about anything except flirting and acting. He was much older than I was, and he also had the answers that were bothering me underneath. So the blacklist was my college, my education. And it was the best education that I could possibly have gotten because the people who were blacklisted, as a group of people, they were the crème de la crème. Wonderful, wonderful men and women who were exciting, who had great ideas, and who expressed ideas that I'd never heard in my life. And I'm not talking politically necessarily. I'm just talking about the fact that they were Renaissance people and they were interesting and so that period was a very enormous period of growth for me.

The essence of the relationship with Arnie was that I was very much in love, that I was very worshipful, the way a student is to a teacher, and that I was very controlled. I was very used to being told what to do and at a certain point gave up my own rights. And we were separated and divorced. He died soon after that. And I've never gone near a relationship that pushed those buttons in me again. And one of the reasons Joey and I have had a friendship that's lasted for twenty years is because it was absolutely opposite to that kind of traditional relationship.

Q: *How do you and your current husband, Joseph Feury, work together?*

A: Very well some of the time, very badly at other times. I mean we argue and fight a lot. He is the producer. He's the keeper of the money. I'm the director and I'm the keeper of the creative focus, although he also has enormous creativity in him. He's a fine artist, and when he goes through a script he knows exactly what's right and wrong with it. So we have within our own house that whole struggle that traditionally goes on between the producer and the director. I'm fighting for the time that I need and for the kinds of things that I need to have, and he's fighting to do it on the budget. But I'm on his side because I want to do it on budget too, and he's on my side because he wants the best quality film. It's the usual... good war.

Q: *How do you feel about starting over as a director?*

A: I'm starting another life as a director. I'm seven years old as a director, whereas I've put in over twenty-five years as an actor. I love starting over. I mean, to me it's very exciting to have to start from the bottom and not be accepted at all, and to fight to be accepted. It's like another motivation. Another obsession. I don't want to be accepted that quickly. I like having to fight for things.

And the thing that I've found in the last ten years — since I stopped being that motivated as an actor — is that those of us actors, women or men, who feel that we're victims in a certain sense, having to wait for a phone call in order to get a job that can sustain us as very, very fine actors, we start to do schlock work. You become a schlock actor. You know, you have to keep balancing, to use your muscles for other things.

Q: *Have you encountered any obstacles in the industry as a direct result of being a woman or an actress?*

A: I wasn't being accepted as a director in Hollywood. It was too soon for people who knew me as an actor to make that transition themselves. I don't think that it was just because I was a woman. I think that it happens with men who are actors too. When you say, "I'm a director now," people say, "Wait a minute." But we came to New York and we started making documentaries.

Ohio Shuffle was the first feature film that Joey and I developed together. We had it set up three times and three times it was knocked down for various reasons. And it was the only project that we had. So we went into such a depression that we couldn't even help each other through the last time because it was everything and everything was gone. All the work. All the time. All the money we had put into it.

When we decided to move to New York, we felt that we had to give ourselves a fresh start. *Ohio Shuffle* was the lesson. We still haven't done *Ohio Shuffle*. *Ohio Shuffle* may be the movie we'll never make. But we're making all our movies in the attempt to make *Ohio Shuffle*. It's like the voyage to Ithaca. That great poem which says, "You never stop at Ithaca — it's the voyage along the way." And so maybe we'll never stop at *Ohio Shuffle*, but all the movies we've made trying to make *Ohio Shuffle* taught us that the more movies we had, the more product we were involved in, the more we could take rejection, disappointment.

Q: *Was the lesson that you learned from* Ohio Shuffle *to have more than one project going at a time?*

A: Yes. Now when someone says, "Oh, we don't want to do this project that you've got," you say, "Okay what about this?" I mean we go with a little pushcart like a peddler and say, "You don't want this, take that. You don't want that, take this." And so we don't ever have that sense anymore of, "Oh God. Our world is crashing in around us. This project is over."

It really gave us a base for operation so that never, never, never would we invest our whole life and blood and everything into one thing.

Q: *What are the qualities of a good director?*

A: Patience. Because as you know, on the set the actual making of the film is a long, gruelling, tedious, usually not thrilling, experience. The hours and hours and hours before the moment of inspiration is the thing that happens in film.

Also, good casting. I worked for Garson Kanin one time. I was in a play and he left us all alone. We were all concerned about why the director didn't direct us and tell us what to do. We had left town with a script that was a little tragedy, and when we came back, it was a little comedy. While we were out of town I asked Garson why he didn't give us direction when we were all so insecure. He said that ninety percent of his work as a director is in casting and he puts those elements together and sees what happens. It was a great lesson for me, and it's one that I think is true not just for me as a director, but for all of us as directors. All that you see is what's in front of the camera, no matter how incredible your vision or your concept.

The instruments, the actors, the art director, and the extraordinary people who put the things in front of the camera are for you to choose. So that the casting for instance of Melvin Douglas and Lila Kedrova in *Tell Me a Riddle* made a magical thing happen. It was so magical that when they did certain scenes together I would be just in back of the camera and the tears would be coming down my face, because what was happening was so remarkable and moving. I remember in that film, when we started it, that Melvin who was playing this kind of irascible Russian-Jewish immigrant who was trying to get his wife to move out of their house said to me, "Don't you think I'm playing this very unsympathetically and that I'll lose the audience? That they won't relate to me?" Later that day he had a scene in which he was trying to climb a ladder in order to fix the roof of the house. Fred Murphy, the cinematographer, started shooting and Melvin tried to climb that ladder. It took two minutes for him to be able to get one foot on the rung and to pull himself up. When he looked at that rooftop, he knew that he couldn't go any further to fix the roof. He came down again to tell his wife that they'd have to move out of the house. I told him that nothing needed to be said. Nothing needed to be explained. That inability of his to care for the house anymore and the time that it took for him to even try to get his foot on the rung said everything to the audience. And it did.

Q: *How do you choose your subject matter?*

A: I get in love. I fall in love with an idea. I fall in love with things that are a reflection of my life, or my relationships, or other things. There's an idea. I want to put it on film. And to get other people to buy that vision and to see what I see and to think enough of it, to put money into it, and to do it — it's hard.

Q: *Was the financing of* Nobody's Child *a difficult task?*

A: It was called a dark film, a depressing film, you know. Writers were fired. Other writers were brought in even though the writers were remarkable because they were always trying to lighten it up. But it's not a light film, and one of the things that was very important to me was that the film did go on the way I wanted it to go on. And it got the audience. I think it was the third most viewed television drama of the year. Now Sven Nykvist shot that film. Alan Hyme edited that film. Michael Small wrote the music. What I tried to do was to bring a fine little feature to television. To say that quality can bring in those kinds of numbers, too. Now to say that, and not say that Marlo Thomas, who has an enormous following, had a very high ability to bring in people to watch a film would be to leave out the star of the crown. Plus the fact that Marlo gave, I think, one of the finest performances that's been done on film in the last couple of years, television or feature. She brought a remarkable quality to it. But this was not *That Girl*. This was not cute. This was a very deep digging of many things that people said they didn't think audiences would want to see. And that's my point, that you can bring a fine quality work to the feature market or to television.

Q: *What is the film* Nobody's Child *about?*

A: *Nobody's Child* is the story of Marie Boulter. The true story of Marie Boulter, who went into a mental institution when she was sixteen. And when she was thirty-six she decided she did not want to be crazy anymore. And she fought for her own sanity in the institution and with the help of a doctor there, step by step found her way out of it. Eventually she ended up in Harvard learning about mental health and came back to the very institution that she was a patient in with a new point-of-view on how to help mental patients and work with them.

Q: *You've won several awards for your directing. How did it feel when you got that first major one from the Directors Guild of America?*

A: It was so unexpected. Unexpected to win. I was so grateful to be nominated because to me it was a club that I never expected to be made a member of. I'd gone there last year when a friend of mine won for making a commercial. And I thought, "Oh gee, it's so nice to be here and I feel sort of outside and I'll never be a part of this." So when I was nominated, I really felt so good about it. So I just had a great time. I got a little drunk. I danced a lot. When they got around to the awards I didn't expect to win. And then when I did I went crazy. I said, "I've worked for you as an actor for many years and I've won many awards as an actor. And in the last seven years it's been a big uphill fight, and my fingernails are bloody from hanging on, and this is my first award as a director." It meant a lot to me.

SEVEN

Randa Haines

Filmography

Under the Sky (1979), PBS TV

Jilting of Granny Weatherall (1979), PBS TV

Hill Street Blues (1982), Episodic TV

Just Pals (1982), ABC TV

Something about Amelia (1984), ABC TV

Children of a Lesser God (1986), Paramount Pictures

The Doctor (1991), Touchstone Pictures

R anda Haines is the acclaimed director of the award-winning film *Children of a Lesser God*. She started in the film business by working at a small production company as a jack-of-all-trades where she made the coffee, opened the mail, and answered the phone. In time she graduated to working on the set and eventually became a continuity girl (someone who makes sure the camera and actors are in the right place). She often found herself working with inexperienced directors and doing their job, which led to her desire to become a director. She applied to the American Film Institute to pursue her goal. To her surprise, she was accepted into the second round of the Directing Workshop for Women. From there she began directing television, including episodes of *Hill Street Blues*. Her talent on these shows did not go unnoticed. She landed an offer to make the controversial television movie *Something about Amelia*. This highly praised, hard-hitting drama focused on the agonizing dilemma of a family's reaction to the discovery of an incestuous relationship. The film earned her an Emmy Award and also secured her reputation for dealing with sensitive issues. Her next directing job was on the feature film *Children of a Lesser God,* starring William Hurt and Marlee Matlin. A tender love story between a headstrong deaf girl and a devoted speech teacher, it received five Academy Award nominations, though Haines was surprisingly overlooked for a nomination as director.

It took five years until she found a picture she was interested in making after *Children of a Lesser God*. In 1991 she undertook *The Doctor*, a controversial look at the corrupt and inadequate medical profession as seen through the eyes of a surgeon, played by William Hurt, who becomes a patient in his hospital after being diagnosed with cancer. Haines believes that there is great power in the messages put on the screen, and only tells stories that she feels are responsible in their message. The result is that she often waits long periods of time between her films, but the films she makes are worth the wait.

Q: *What appealed to you when you read the script for* The Doctor?

A: The aspect that really appealed to me was the story of a person who goes through a complete transformation. And the plot was interesting — a doctor becoming a patient, and having his whole point of view turned upside-down. He starts out as someone who has a real fear of intimacy and is only comfortable when he's in control. He's chosen an aspect of medicine where the patients are unconscious all the time, so he can really feel in control. And by having his world turned upside-down, by becoming the patient, he loses control and enters into intimate contact with other people.

Q: *How did you go about creating a comfortable atmosphere for the actors to work in?*

A: I did a tremendous amount of research. And I encouraged the actors to do a lot of research. I made arrangements for them to meet every different type of doctor. And we built a fabulous set. Ninety-eight percent of what you see taking place in the hospital is a set. So all of that helps, the research and the sets, and the degree of accuracy that I committed myself to achieving on the set by having consultants there throughout.

The actors have a safe sense of reality when you pay attention to detail that way. Also, many of the doctors you see around the operating tables are real doctors. So the performers were challenged to be as convincing as the real people, and the real people were challenged to reach a level of performance equal to the believability of the performers. All of that helps set the atmosphere.

Q: *You cast William Hurt in the lead. He also played the lead in your film* Children of a Lesser God. *How was it working with him again?*

A: Better than the first time [laugh]. I called him and told him about the material. I knew him well enough to make a very good guess that he would be interested in it. He committed to it when he read the script. And he knew me, so there was an element of trust there, in that we had previously worked together, and that we'd done very good work together. That's the good thing about working with people again — you already know how to communicate, and you have a level of trust, especially if the work is good.

Q: *Had you always wanted to be a director?*

A: My first job in film was for a production company in New York. A non-union company, which meant that I had to learn a lot of different things and actually do them, not just watch other people do them. Of course I had to open the mail and make the coffee in the morning. Terrible coffee. I think I also got to work in the editing room syncing the dailies. I started working with sound effects on documentaries. I was fortunate because I worked with these two men who loved to teach. That was a great opportunity. But after about a year they had to lay me off because they didn't have enough money to pay me anymore. After that I got a job working as a script supervisor on a very low budget film where they couldn't afford to hire anybody who had ever done it before.

So I kind of figured the job out as a I went along. I always managed to stay a step ahead of the director who knew less than I did. After that I started working as a script supervisor and learning more and more about it. I did that for almost ten years in New York. What happened was, about five years into that process of working as a script supervisor, I began thinking about directing myself. People were often coming up to me on the set and saying, "You should be directing." I was often working with first-time directors on their very first film. Helping them. Thinking along with them, and trying to anticipate problems. Very often I'd be whispering suggestions in their ear, like, "Maybe you could try blah, bla, bla." And then they'd say, "Okay. We're going to try blah, bla, bla." And I'd think, "Well, gee, I'd like to say that out loud myself, and see if I could do this." But it took another five years before I had the opportunity to really say it out loud myself and that was through the directing workshop for women at the AFI.

Q: *What was that workshop like?*

A: It was very interesting. I was in the second group. It had seemed to me that everyone in this program was a movie star.

Everybody had an Oscar, or their husband had an Oscar. And I thought, "How will I ever get into this program?" But I wrote them a very passionate letter about the situation I found myself in as a frustrated script supervisor, and explained that I didn't know how to make the transition. So I got in. But I still thought I was the token unknown among all these movie stars. For example, in the group was Anne Bancroft and Marilyn Bergman, a lyricist who had many Oscars, and a lot of other very interesting people. But even so we managed to help each other with the different skills we brought to the workshop. I remember Marilyn calling me one day with a screen direction problem. She had shot something right to left, left to right, and was wondering how she was ever going to make it work. I came in and watched her dailies and helped her figure it out because that was my background. I could see how to make something that wouldn't work, work. On the other hand, she looked at my film and really helped with how to approach the music. That was a wonderful cross fertilization of experiences.

Q: *How did you get involved with* Children of a Lesser God, *and what attracted you to the material?*

A: A television movie I directed called *Something about Amelia* had just aired around the time that I was approached with *Children*. After the airing of *Amelia*, the film received a great deal of attention for its subject matter and for the tasteful way in which it was done. So, as the director, this response brought a lot of attention to me. It was my first movie for television and the only one I'd done. *Children of a Lesser God* had been a successful play and had been in development for a couple of years at Universal Studios, not at Paramount where it was eventually made. And there had been a couple of directors involved and a couple of drafts written and it had just not become a movie yet. They started looking for another director and my agent sent me the material to look at. The thing that interested me most about *Children* when I first read the material was the potential to tell a story about communication. I had some very strong feelings about it. About the struggles all human beings face in reaching each other. We all have layers of protection built up around us that make us unable to see, unable to hear, unable to feel. How

Randa Haines directing *Children of a Lesser God*, with Marlee Matlin

we get past those layers of fear, how we finally reach each other, that subject interests me the most I think. The whole theme of communication is very much a part of *Children of a Lesser God*. I think back now and a lot of other things I've done seem to be about that as well.

What's exciting about what has happened with the film is that it has communicated a lot of different things to people. It certainly has created an awareness about deaf people, and that's a wonderful side benefit of the film. I've gotten a lot of letters from people who tell me that it affected their relationships — with their lover, their husband, their mate. In some cases they said they really talked to each other for the first time in years. You can't ask for much more than that in terms of reaching an audience.

I also hope that the film has another benefit which is perhaps a greater openness to women as directors of films that are perhaps out of the traditional genre that women have been working in during the last few years. Teen comedies, for example. *Children* was a very prestigious project and has had a big commercial success. I hope it's had the effect to open the door just a little bit further for women.

Q: *How do you choose your material?*

A: I think that I have been extremely lucky in the material that has come my way, that it hasn't fallen into any particular box. That people have not looked at me as, "Oh, a woman director. That means she can only do films about kids, about this or that."

I have also waited long periods of time between the things I have done. I've waited till the right thing came along. I was offered other features before *Children*. Teen comedies. And that's something I just don't relate to, don't feel. My teenage years were very different from the way most of these films are told. I didn't go to the prom. I didn't care about the prom. It was not an issue in my life who was taking me to the prom. So a movie about that is not something I can bring something to. But a film about people who are wounded and struggle with their emotions, that's the kind of material that interests me. That's where I was in my teenage years and where my life has been. That's what I have to bring to material. I've waited till things have come along that I have something to say about, that I could do well.

Q: *What was it like leaping to a big budget picture after directing only one television movie?*

A: When I began *Children of a Lesser God* I knew this was a respectable budget. This was a major style of film. It was extremely difficult material. I believed there was potential to make a film that would reach a lot of people, not just a special art film, or a special little film about people who are different from the rest of us. I didn't see it that way. So I felt an enormous responsibility. But you can't think about that when you're working. You don't think about how many millions of dollars are sitting on your shoulders. What you think about is just making each scene the best it can be. Doing the best you can do with each little increment. Making it the best it can be. If you stop for a second and think about how much money is on your shoulders or the weight of this responsibility, you get paralyzed. Instead you just have to keep doing the work and stay really focused. My involvement on *Children of a Lesser God* from the time I started to the time the film opened was three years. It was the kind of material that was so rich it kept my vision clearly focused on it. My feelings about it were so strong that I was able to keep my vision that whole time and never stopped to panic about what other people would think or how much money it cost or any other factors.

Q: *How do you work with actors?*

A: When you're working with an actor like William Hurt, or the process of working with any actor really, you try to build a relationship of trust. You can't be intimidated by what someone has done. You can be respectful of it, but if you start to be intimidated you've lost your ground. You're in there as partners and you have to do the work together and give whatever that actor needs from you. Every actor you work with has different needs. Some need a great deal of loving and nurturing and an atmosphere that makes them feel safe. Others feel just the opposite, they need to feel danger all the time. They need to feel conflict all the time and you have to provide that too, even if it's against your style. I've had that experience and I'm not a screamer, but if somebody needs that from me, I adapt and create an atmosphere that will make their work grow.

Q: *Do you think you've encountered additional obstacles by being a woman film director?*

A: I think in the film industry getting at directing is the hardest thing there is, for a man or a woman. I think in the last few years it has been harder for women than it has for men, but for someone who's determined enough, they will get a chance. I think for me, it felt like it was taking a long time. Now, when I look back it feels like everything happened in its proper time. But there were days, many days, when I despaired a great deal, and woke up with tears streaming down my face thinking, "I've wasted my life. I've invested all this time here and it's not going to go anywhere. This has been just a terrible mistake." Usually the day after a moment of incredible despair, of touching bottom, a great transition would occur and something positive would happen. Things would start rolling. That happened to me many times at each level. It takes an enormous amount of stamina to make a career happen. Most of that is inner belief in yourself. It keeps you making all the phone calls, and getting up every day even if you get up crying. If you just keep going through the motions, someday you'll be doing it. You also need a lot of friends to support you, and who believe in you. It's hard. It's very hard. But if you can stay focused maybe it will happen.

Q: *Do you think films should be used for political change?*

A: I think that film is an incredibly powerful medium, and I think that filmmakers have a tremendous responsibility. The images that you put up on that screen go out into people's minds and stay there. I know for myself that I've seen things on screen that I wish I could erase from my memory. Things I don't want inside me. I think we have to be really careful about how we tell stories, because the impact on people is enormous. *Something about Amelia,* for example. That film was seen by sixty million people in one night. It had the potential to really frighten a lot of people, children certainly. I felt an enormous responsibility to tell that story in a way that would perhaps motivate people to take some action, to get out instead of being paralyzed with fear. Especially people who found themselves in similar situations. In fact there were thousands and thousands and thousands of phone calls and letters from children who were in a similar incestuous nightmare. Also, letters from mothers who finally admitted what was happening in their households. And from fathers who were actual perpetrators. I never expected anything like that to happen. That was an extraordinary experience to feel that sort of response and to feel that we had in some way affected people's lives in a positive way. So, there's great power there. Great power.

Q: *Did you have any female role models when you started?*

A: When I was a script supervisor I don't think I ever met a woman director. People would come up to me and say, "You should be a director." I'd think, "Gee, that's a great idea, but how do I do it?" I didn't have any role models or anyone to focus on. I can remember thinking at the time, "There aren't any women making films." I'm sure it affected my waiting.

Q: *Do you feel that the film industry is a sexist business?*

A: People always ask me in interviews, "What are the terrible things that happen? Where's the prejudice been? Have you seen that because you're a woman, they wouldn't want to listen to you or give you jobs or whatever?" Either I have been very lucky and not encountered that very much, or I have decided unconsciously to put blinders on. I've tuned it out if I felt it on the set. If you let in that negativity, "Oh she's a woman, she can't make up her mind," whatever the things that they say are, it drains your energy and it drains every ounce of strength you have in order just to get the job done. I always felt if you can just let the work speak for itself, eventually it will do the trick.

I think that's what has started to happen in the last few years. I don't feel that negativity any more and when I do, I shut it out. I would advise anyone else to do that. You can't let it shift your focus or take your energy away. Don't waste time being angry. Do your job. Come prepared. Know what you want, and have a clear sense of how your day should go. That's what a crew wants from a director. They want to finish the day and go home, and if they sense that you're prepared and know what you want to do, they'll go with you.

Q: *Do you think there is a specific female point of view?*

A: I don't think that we will know for quite some time if there is such a thing as a female point of view on screen. I think that only once we have seen enough movies by enough women, and stories they have chosen to make, not just jobs they were allowed to have, but stories they have nurtured and brought to the screen themselves, then maybe we can look at this whole body of work and say, "Yes, there is a feminine perspective." I suspect there won't be that point of view. I suspect we will see as many action films as sensitive films. We will see every kind of film coming from women as we do from male directors. I think that would be a really exciting thing to discover, because there are so many different kinds of women and so many different stories to tell.

Q: *Do you feel a responsibility to create positive images on film for women to identify with?*

A: I think we all do. I think we all have a responsibility, men and women, to create images on the screen that men and women and children and human beings can relate to. That we tell stories about things that people go through. Those are the kind of films I want to make. Films that help people feel something. That they laugh and cry and have some identification with the characters. I think that if you have characters that are really true, their gender is less important. Men and women can identify with real human beings on the screen. And we don't see them as often as we might. I think that those are the kind of films that can really reach people.

Q: *What are you working on now?*

A: I'm set to shoot a film this fall for Warner Brother's. At the moment it's called *Wrestling Ernest Hemingway*, but I have a feeling that the studio's going to change the title. And the one I hope to do after that is the one that is closest to my heart. It's a love story about an American woman and a Latin American man who meet in a salsa club in Los Angeles. Right now I'm developing a script. I've commissioned a novelist, Judith Freeman, to write a short story on which to base the screenplay. The idea is to have her write it, based on my story concept.

Q: *Any advise to aspiring filmmakers?*

A: That's difficult because there's no single clear path to follow. The main thing I think is perseverance and a belief in yourself. Surround yourself with supportive people who believe in you and can help you stay strong. Then just follow up every lead, and keep working at it.

EIGHT

Amy Heckerling

Filmography

Modern Times (1973), NYU, Short

High Finance (1974), NYU, Short

Getting It Over With (1977), AFI, Short

Fast Times at Ridgemount High (1982), Universal

Johnny Dangerously (1984), Twentieth Century-Fox

National Lampoon's European Vacation (1985), Warner Brothers

Look Who's Talking (1989), Tri-Star Pictures

Look Who's Talking Too (1991), Tri-Star Pictures

The blockbuster hit of 1989 *Look Who's Talking*, a contemporary romantic comedy told from the point of view of baby Mikey, was penned and directed by native New Yorker Amy Heckerling. She grew up in Queens and the Bronx, and decided to become a film director while attending Manhattan's School of Art and Design. She graduated from New York University with two successful shorts to her credit, and relocated to Los Angeles in 1975 where she attended the American Film Institute. Her half hour short made there, *Getting It Over With*, starred Glynnis O'Connor as a nineteen-year-old virgin who did not want to be a virgin at twenty. Considered for an Academy Award nomination, it was her calling card to the industry.

A producer friend, Art Linson, offered Heckerling her first feature, *Fast Times at Ridgemount High*. The teen comedy, written by Cameron Crowe and starring a then unknown Sean Penn, had an affecting charm that was hard to resist. A huge success both artistically and commercially, it thrust the first time director into the limelight. On the heels of *Fast Times*, she directed Michael Keaton in the gangster spoof comedy *Johnny Dangerously*. Before that film was released, she took the helm on her third feature, *National Lampoon's European Vacation*, starring Chevy Chase and Beverly D'Angelo. The slapstick comedy became one of the top grossers of 1986.

Formerly married to director, writer, producer Neal Israel, it was their daughter, born in 1987, who inspired Heckerling to write *Look Who's Talking*. She remembers looking at her daughter in her baby seat and wondering what thoughts were going on in her head. This prompted her to create a voice over to express the inner thoughts of baby Mikey which were brought to life by the voice of Bruce Willis. A huge box office success, she promptly started work on the sequel, *Look Who's Talking Too*. A director and screenwriter known for her comedic flair, Heckerling is one of the few female directors who has worked regularly within Hollywood's motion picture machinery.

Q: *How did the original idea for* Look Who's Talking *come about?*

A: I'd had a baby. And I spent some time developing a TV series based on *Fast Times at Ridgemount High*, but it didn't get picked up. I thought, now what am I going to do? I was having a lot of fun with the baby, so I got the idea and I got the script together and went around to pitch it. I don't like pitching, but Tri Star picked it up.

Q: *Two women claimed to have given you their script with the concept of* Look Who's Talking. *What happened there?*

A: They say that every movie that makes over one hundred million has its law suit, so we had ours. I'd never been through anything like that. It was a very Kafkaesque experience. I don't know if you ever read *The Trial*: a guy wakes up in the morning and people say you're guilty and now you have to go and deal with all this legal stuff. Well, that's what it was like. And when I did the sequel we started a deposition of discovery. It took forever. I went off to do the movie and when I got back it was settled out of court, apparently amicably.

Q: *Tell me about the financing of your first project.*

A: The first thing I ever wrote, in my life, I did when I got out of film school. Warner Brothers picked it up and they were going to make it. They were very excited, but by the time I handed it in, there were new executives there, and these new executives didn't like it. Now by that time, I had sort of established a relationship with executives at Universal. So I showed it to them and they picked it up. But again by the time I handed it in, there were also new people, and again they decided not to make it. And then it went to MGM, and they were definitely going to make it. So, they said, "Just shorten it." So I shortened it and then we're finally making the film. We're two weeks away from shooting. I have an entire cast. I have a crew. I have the locations picked. The sets are all built. They were making costumes, and props, and the actors go on strike. So they told me to just keep working because as soon as the strike ended, we'd be making the film. The producer and I worked all summer. It got down to me knowing every single color everybody was going to wear, and what color every wall was going to be. I knew in my head how every line of dialogue was going to be said. I knew too much about how to make this movie. So, the strike kept going on and on, and they said, "Don't worry, as soon as it's over." Then one day they said, "Oh-oh, the strike's been going on a long time and we're going to drop some of our films." And me being the sort of new kid, with this little budget film, they told me, "Well, it looks like we're not going to make this film."

Then a number of people came in and said, "We're going to make the movie. We'll put in half the money." So I had a number of halves of the money, but no two halves equaled a whole. Then I went off and I did *Fast Times*, and *Johnny Dangerously*. Periodically, in between those other films, new places would crop up. At one point, Orion tried. So I kept having meetings on this script. Then I did *Vacation* and I had a baby. Meanwhile, somebody else comes and says, "We raised money for that script. Now rewrite it." By this time I have eight drafts, so I said, "What do I do with it?" Because I have eight drafts. They said, "Just do what you think is best." So now I'm in a position of rewriting it again, not knowing which way to go with it, but knowing that there's money there waiting for it to be made. And this has been a process that started as soon as I got out of film school. So it's been eight years of this one movie that never dies and never gets made. And some day maybe it'll get made, but it'll be very weird to see what it looks like.

I'm currently doing another rewrite. Columbia Pictures is paying me to write it again. It's like a perpetual motion machine. It's called *My Kind of Guy*. I was going through the old drafts and was surprised to see how much my point of view has changed over the years. You know, it's about relationships and one year it's completely negative, and the next year it's like this is the answer. Now two studios later there's even yet another point of view. One year it's about lowering your standards, and another year it's stick to your dreams. So it's hard to say what it will finally be about.

Q: *How did you discover the script for* Fast Times at Ridgemount High?

A: I knew Art Linson who was also at Universal. He had an office right above my office and we knew a lot of similar people. He had shown me other scripts that he was working on. I would tell him what I thought of the different scripts and he would tell me what he thought of what I was doing. Then one day he showed me *Fast Times*, which I think was called *Stairway to Heaven* then. I would tell him what I thought about it, and then he surprised me by asking if I wanted to do it. That was a very big shock because I had absolutely no idea that he was thinking of me in those terms. Of hiring me to direct a movie. I was going, "Oh my God. Do I want to do this?" I was writing something that I really loved, and I thought, "If I do that, then I won't finish this. If I drop it now, it'll go away forever." I kept thinking about *Fast Times* and I thought, "If I don't do it, somebody else will, and if somebody else does it, I'll just be miserable." I loved Cameron's script, and I also loved Cameron's book. When I read that material, I thought this is very real. It just knocks you over compared to the other scripts that are floating around. And so my decision became clear. I knew I had to make the movie.

Q: *What did you like about the script when you read it?*

A: Cameron Crowe went to a high school and very accurately recorded and got to know all these kids. He put down this absolutely real account, non-judgmental, and with a lot of love for all these people and what they were going through. Surprisingly enough it all works as a story. We all tried to stay true to the spirit.

Q: *Tell me about your first day on the set of a studio picture.*

A: So there I was, making the movie. It was my first day, and I had to do a drive-by. It was my very first shot. There's a car, and it had to go from left to right. And I'm thinking, "How am I going to do that?" It's like, how big is the car? Should I start with the car and pan with it? Should I just let the car pass through the frame? Or should I pan all the way with the car? All of a sudden the possibilities were far too endless. I didn't know how anyone

Amy Heckerling, directing *Fast Times at Ridgemount High*, with Sean Penn

had ever shot a car going by. Then we did it and it was over. And all of a sudden it was okay, and I thought, "Now I can shoot the girl standing looking at the car, the close-up of the girl looking at the car and the guy." All the other shots just came because I had gotten rid of this car.

Q: *What is your approach to working with large crews?*

A: Everybody always says, "How do you deal with these crew people?" As though crews were wild gorillas, and teamsters, and scary, and they're going to yell at you, and they're not going to listen. But the reality is that you interview a lot of people, and you hire the ones that you like the best. You have many meetings before you're actually on a set and you've already established relationships with your key people. On the set you meet the people that they're working with and you're all working together. You have your job to do and you do it. You've decided to work with these people because you've liked what they've done, and you like how you get along with them, and then there's no problem.

Q: *Because of its popularity, what happened to your career after* Fast Times at Ridgemount High *came out?*

A: After *Fast Times* came out, I had a lot of scripts offered to me that had to do with preppies, because they thought, "You did high school. You could do school." And they thought there was going to be this preppy trend, that everybody would think it was adorable to be rich and young and wear madras shorts. I couldn't relate to that. I didn't go to prep school, obviously. I didn't see what was so cute about being young and rich. And my mother had said, "Don't do another high school movie and don't do a girl movie, and don't let them pigeonhole you." So I was turning down all these preppie movies. Then I read *Johnny Dangerously,* which was a comedy about gangsters. It was guys and guns, and was very rowdy and dirty. I thought, "This is different. They're not going to think of me as 'the-girl-loses-virginity' if they see this."

Q: *How did that turn out?*

A: Well, here we are working on this film, and we all think it's very funny because we know the references for the humor, which are the 1930s Warner Brothers films. I was also hoping that all these other gangster movies coming out before it would do well — *Once Upon a Time in America, Scarface,* and *City Heat.* I thought all these things would bring back the gangsters. But it didn't quite work out that way. So when we brought it out, here was this satire based on things that nobody remembered. So I thought, "Now what?" and before it came out I knew I had to do something fast, so I did *European Vacation.* And that came out and did well. So when people were saying, "Uh-oh, *Johnny Dangerously* didn't do well," I already had something else in the can. I remained this question mark. So I like to stay away from what they think you should do. And try to stay away from pigeonholes.

Q: *Do you find that you get typecast because you are a woman?*

A: Every time you do something people would like to say, "Oh, you do that, so let's put you in that slot." If they think you can do films with people against their lockers and the girls losing their virginity, then you can't do a thing with guns. Or if you can do something with people pulling their pants down, then you can't do something where people cry. You can do this, but you can't do that. So I feel this desperation to hop away from where they want you to go.

Q: *Do you think there are certain problems that are specific to being a woman in the film industry, in Hollywood?*

A: Just to keep my sanity, I have to not think about that. Because if I'm going to say "I am a woman, with women, in the women's group, on the women's list," then I'm in deep trouble. I just have to think of what I want to do, what I want to express, and not think about what this town thinks of me as a woman. I don't think about what's hot, and what's not. As soon as you start with that, you're dead. That's not to say you don't see the realities of the situation, but as soon as you start thinking in terms of I'm a woman, I'm a Jew, I'm a New Yorker, I grew up poor, or I grew up rich, I'm this, or I'm that, then I think you're pigeonholing yourself.

Q: *What are the qualities that make a good director?*

A: There's a pamphlet that Elia Kazan wrote about what makes a good director. And if you read it you'd say, yeah well, everything. You have to know about lenses, you have to know about dance, you have to know about diseases, you have to know about the world, you have to know about cars, you have to know about everything. I mean it lists everything you could ever know about. So if you know about all of this stuff, that's what makes a good director.

But basically, if you love the characters that you're portraying, and you have some sense of how to tell a story, how to amuse people, how to make people cry, how to scare people, whatever you want to do, if you can get that across, you're okay.

Q: *How do you manage your time between a film career and a family?*

A: If you're really worried about any career, you're going to push a lot of things back. You're not going to get married at the age of twenty, or have your first kid then. You're going to change your time schedule. And that's not to say it's a sacrifice. I think it helps.

Q: *Has the situation for woman directors changed since you started?*

A: When I was going to film school, my father would always say, "Yeah right, a woman director." He'd never heard of such a thing. And when I'd try to say, "Well what about Elaine May?" he'd say, "Who else?" And I couldn't think of anyone else. If I was in film school now, I assume that I could say, "What about Claudia Weill? What about Lisa Gottlieb? What about Martha Coolidge? What about Donna Deitch? What about Joyce Chopra? What about several people?" I think that's a big difference.

But as far as the situation that there is still X amount of women who would like to direct who haven't had the opportunity, or the fact that the Directors Guild only has one-millionth of a percentage that are women, then it's still fairly depressing. But still, there are a lot more women directing now than when I started.

Q: *Do you consider* Fast Times at Ridgemount High *to be a film with a definite female perspective?*

A: Well what happened on *Fast Times* was a good cross-sampling of male and female perspectives. There were two girls and four boys who were primary characters. Cameron and I went through what really happens to everybody in the story, and what would be good dramatically to wrap the people up. Because it was a slice of life film, a year in the life of all these kids, we both had to start pulling things in. We combined a few characters, and then we had to start pulling things out of our own lives. We had a wonderful couple of weeks where we went through all the information that was in the book, that was in Cameron's research notes from the book, and that was in our own lives. We took these characters that were real and kept giving them everything that we could find that we thought would work for them. So there's a lot of the real girls that he knew, and there's a lot of me, and a lot of him. I think that is clear in the movie, the male and female points-of-view. We're both in there, both coming up with the stuff.

Q: *What are you going to do next? Are you looking for any particular type of material?*

A: I think just to be true to myself. And I don't want to do anything like what I've done before. I'm writing a couple of things that I really want to do. I want to do more things that I've written. I feel like I got real anxious to be in the business, for people to say, "There's Amy Heckerling. She's making this movie." There's this rush to find material that will get made rather than asking yourself, "Does this express how I feel?" And it's hard to sit with blank pieces of paper wondering, "What is she going to say next?" And if you run into one of these agents floating around in restaurants and they say, "What're you doing?" and you go, "Well, I'm writing," they say, "Uh huh, so are the waiters." It's harder, and you don't feel that big shock, but that's what I want to do next.

Q: *What type of films do you hope to make?*

A: I don't want to do a movie that a bunch of critics say is great, but it makes no money. And I don't want people to go to the Beverly Center and see it and go, "That stunk." I want to make movies that people stand in line for, and they go back again. And I don't work independently. I go out and pitch things. I always seem to land at some studio, where I'm pitching a project within the big studio machinery.

Q: *What is your latest project?*

A: I've got a script in at Disney, and we have a green light on it, but there are a few things that are still up in the air, so we're going to see what will happen. And there's a sequel being mounted for *Look Who's Talking* [three], but I'm not writing or directing it. I'll be supervising it with the other producer. I'm trying to move away from movies with kids because having a kid, every moment is all encompassing. It really consumes you. At least on a movie you can take a break between shots if everything is going okay, but every second with a baby you're wondering, "Are they okay? What are they doing?"

Q: *Any advice for aspiring filmmakers?*

A: It's different for everybody. It's hard to describe how one person can end up making certain things for them work while another person will make completely different things work for them. There are a lot of things about Hollywood show business that I block out so I can stay in my own dream world, because I don't like that stuff. For other people, they might survive on the game, the aggression and all of that. So what works for me is not necessarily something I could recommend for anyone else.

NINE

Micheline Lanctôt

Filmography

A Token Gesture (1975), Animated Short, NFB

L'Homme à Tout Faire (1980), Les Films René Malo

Sonantine (1984), Les Films René Malo

Onzième Spéciale (1988), TV Drama

Deux Actrices (1993), Max Films Communications

Micheline Lanctôt, award winning Canadian actress and director, was born in the Eastern Townships of Quebec and raised in Outremont, a prestigious area in Montreal. She always knew she wanted to be in the arts. Her love for cartoons led her to the National Film Board of Canada where she studied animation. In the early 1970s, she began working in film as a cell animator.

Gilles Carles, who had an office at the NFB, launched her acting career when he cast her in his film, *La vraie nature de Bernadette* (*The True Nature of Bernadette*). The role of Bernadette earned Lanctôt a Canadian Film Award (now the Genie Awards). She is best known to international audiences for her role as Yvette (Richard Dreyfuss's girlfriend) in *The Apprenticeship of Duddy Kravitz*. She fondly thinks of that role as her favorite performance.

Lanctôt fell in love with the film's director, Ted Kotcheff, and followed him to Hollywood. After five years, she left the relationship, said goodbye to Hollywood, and returned to Montreal to resume her career. While attempting to sell a script she'd written, she decided to direct it instead. *L'Homme à Tout Faire* (*The Handyman*), made for $500,000, showed at Cannes to favorable reviews, and picked up six Genie nominations at home. Believing that her talents are put to good use as a director, Lanctôt continues to pursue writing and directing along with her acting career. Known for her strong often controversial opinions, she does not hesitate to speak her mind.

Q: *What was the main theme of your first feature film,* The Handyman?

A: *The Handyman* was a film about a man basically. There was nothing more than that. It was just aiming to be a portrait of a certain type of character, and I don't know whether it succeeds or not, but certainly the character was appealing. I'm afraid of talking better about the film than what it is, which you always do when you have hindsight on a film. I have to bring myself back to why I made this film. I had met such a character when I was living in Los Angeles, and I was amazed by his total lack of defence system. He was an immigrant, a Czech immigrant. He was totally helpless in America because he didn't know the rules. He didn't know them, and he didn't want to learn. He was quite a fabulous character. Originally, I had written him as a Czech immigrant, then I thought that considering the state of filmmaking in Quebec, it would be impossible. Nobody would accept that. So I transposed him into a Québécois context and I made him a man from out of town. I gave him very strong, indigenous Quebec traits, and went from there. That's all the film really wanted to say. I felt very close to that kind of character, and that's what it's about.

Q: *Did you run into any difficulties in financing* The Handyman *because you were a woman?*

A: It was quite amazing. I was on the full wind of women's pictures, which riles me to no end, because I don't like tags of any kind. But it was the kind of year when women were being considered for films, and they were sort of blindly throwing money away on any woman who had a script. I profited from that I guess, and the fact that I worked behind the camera as a film animator, and had quite a reputation as an actress. Those things made it easier for the film to be considered for production. They did object because I had never directed before. I had to put up with a godfather director who ensured he would finish the picture should I fail as a director. And he didn't have to. I finished the picture. I don't remember encountering the usual run of inane readings, and with comedies it can go on forever. There could be five readers and four like it and one doesn't, or five other readers, where three like it and two don't. Three could like the beginning, two like the end, two don't like the middle part, things like that. But that's sort of standard practice here. It's a democratic industry.

Q: *What was your experience like directing your first feature?*

A: I went through that picture not knowing what it was about. I just went through it with sheer gusto I guess. Chutspa, as they say. I realized half way through the film how hard it was directing films. It wasn't what I'd experienced as an actress. My only real plus was that working with the actors was easy. But anything that had to do with where to put the camera was total anguish and panic. Half way through the film, it sort of came together and I said, "Ah, yes. This is how it's done." The film got easier for me as I went along. I think that the last part of the film is better directed than the first part, because I sort of understood how it worked. The second film was worse, because then you know what you're getting yourself into, and you know the mistakes that you can make. But the first one wasn't intimidating, because it was folly. I wouldn't recommend that anyone should ever go on a set and say, "I'm going to direct a picture, and here I go," because, whew, it's really hard.

Q: *Why did you move from acting to directing?*

A: It was never a conscious desire. I'd lived with directors before and I saw the insane kind of life that they lived. I wasn't attracted to it as a profession. What I liked doing best was writing, and I had written a lot while I was in Los Angeles. I had written the script for *The Handyman* without any intention to direct it. But when I showed it to the producer he felt that it was such a strongly personal film that I should direct it. I went mmhhh, and thought, yeah, it's a good idea. Subsequently, when I was directing, I realized that it was far more suited to my personality than acting was. I tend to want to change the world. I don't submit to it very easily. So directing was good for me in that respect. It made me the boss over a lot of people, and it gave me the chance to control the actual film. But there was no burning desire to become a director.

Q: *Was it more difficult to convince others to let you direct because of your acting background?*

A: No, it was the opposite. It gave me credibility. Why? I don't know, because the two are totally different. You cannot be qualified to be a director because you're an actress. There's no cause and effect relationship. It's mostly the reverse that's true. I don't think actors make very good directors. Directors make better actors than actors make directors. But funny enough, it didn't play against me. It played for me. They assumed that I had knowledge of the set, which is true. Acting gives you working knowledge of a set. But it doesn't give you directing talent.

And it's a whole new set of rules that you have to face. I remember when I was an actress on *Duddy Kravitz*, we kept bitching, as actors do, saying "Oh, there's nothing to directing." The greatest lesson I ever had was when Ted Kotcheff said to me and Richard Dreyfuss, "You want to direct? I'm walking out of this room. You have an hour to set yourself up, do it, show it to me and put it in the can." And he walked out. So Richard and I went, "You stand there when I do this," and, "Well no, you put that there," and, "No, we'll start there," and, "You go there." We did this for an hour, because we didn't have the whole picture in our minds. We didn't have the previous shot in mind. We had no sense of continuity. And we were totally mortified. We sort of sat there and waited for Ted to come back. When he came back he went, "What? Have we got a scene?" And we said, "No we're sorry." It was the best, and most economical way of putting an actor in their place, and without actually saying "You shut up and do your thing," and, "If you're an actor then act, don't try to direct." It's true. You can't just improvise yourself for the director.

Q: *Did you feel objectified as an actress?*

A: Well, yes. But I don't object to it, because it's part of directing. But some directors are more clever at it than others. Most directors that I've worked with weren't bad in staging actors, but were hopeless in dealing with them.

I don't like directors who try to make me believe that I'm not an object and that I'm the sole force of his thoughts, because its not true. I know it as an actor. I feel it every day on the set.

There's a very hard line for a director to walk, as far as film actors are concerned. They constantly have to make actors feel they're totally vital to the picture when actually they have ten thousand more important things to think about.

Q: *Did you move into directing partly because there were no good women's roles?*

A: Everybody knows it. I'm just repeating a cliché. It's very hard to find good women's parts. I used to take on any part, because I liked acting. Now I don't. If I'm going to go through the pains of acting again, I want to make it worth my while. Role models have changed so much in the past twenty years. Yet it's still very hard for the public to identify with the female equivalent of a male leading role. The change has been brought up on the upper layers, but the bottom layers of the population have not evolved that much. There are a lot of feminists who said, "Men only write about men." It's not true. They know that if they write about certain types of women, the films won't be seen or the audiences won't be able to identify with the characters. The most daring character they make, like in *Romancing The Stone,* for example, is a mousy lady that the people can relate to. She's not adventurous in the full sense of the word.

I always fancied myself as adventurous, and that's the types of parts I like to play. They're not written. If you write them, the role is too far away from what the average public thinks. It becomes a problem of credibility more than the character. It's very hard, and it's a sign of the times. The roles are changing and it's still very hard to get a grasp on what can be said universally about women. You don't want to say something for ten percent of the population. You want to say it for ninety percent. So you have to say what they know and what they can relate to, hoping that they can advance all at the same time. It's very hard. It's complicated. It makes me very skeptical about going back to acting, because I really don't think acting is interesting for women.

Q: *You spent some time living in Los Angeles. What was your impression of Hollywood?*

A: I can say it in one word. Yuk! There's nothing more to say about Hollywood. I didn't go there for career purposes. I followed Ted because I was in love. I can safely say, notwithstanding the personal relationship, they were the six worst years of my life. It's a place I cannot live. I had no existence whatsoever. None. When I say none, people don't believe me. They say "None?" None. To the point of being trotted on at parties.

People step on your feet because if you're not there for them, you don't exist. If you're not somebody that has a name above the title, that they can bargain with, you don't exist. I found that totally impossible to take. Totally incompatible with my set of personal values. Hence, I had to leave. After three years I started commuting and then when I could no longer stand that, I just left and came back. But I didn't come back with the tail between my legs, I just felt it was an unhealthy living environment. I hated everything about Los Angeles — the climate, the place, the everything. There's something totally plastic about life in Los Angeles. Other people survive very well. It takes an enormous amount of courage to live there. An enormous amount.

Q: *So then, would you ever agree to direct a picture for a major studio in Hollywood?*

A: No, not unless it was on my terms. I will never work on their terms. I don't like their terms. I've witnessed things that are unspeakable there, in terms of trying to get a job. I wouldn't like to lose whatever dignity I have. I don't want to leave it on the floors of Los Angeles. It's really a place that leaves you totally stripped of anything human.

In order to succeed there, you really have to abdicate everything that I hold dear — dignity, honor, honesty, anything. If you want to succeed there, you have to do away with it. If you're a fairly decent person, you cannot make it in Hollywood. It's unfortunate, but it's true.

Q: The Handyman *was invited to Cannes. What was your experience like?*

A: I'm not a festival girl. I don't like these things. That whole side of movie making never appealed to me. I find I'm not very comfortable in situations like that. It's such an artificial recognition. I

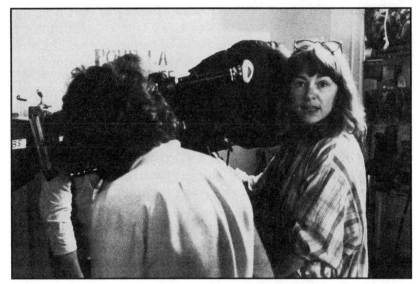

Micheline Lanctôt on the set of
L'Homme à Tout Faire

was never seduced by it. I just see it for what it is. And I don't find it very appealing. It's really political. I don't mind being judged by people I respect, but I do dislike being evaluated by people that I have no respect for. And I don't particularly cater to that kind of system. I know it's necessary. I know it's promotional. I know it's important for a picture's life. But the less I have to do with it, the better.

Q: *What do you think about the film industry in Canada?*

A: It's an industry. If I could find a way to make films outside of the industry, I would. I don't feel at ease in an industrial context. I wouldn't mind making money, but it's not my goal in life. Some people get into movies because they want to make money. Fine. Or they want to be famous.

I got into movies because I like to make films. And unfortunately, there's such a gap between the likable side of film and the hateful side of film, that I find it hard to reconcile. When I make a picture, I'm happy. I like working on the set. I like making a picture. I like inventing things for film. But everything that goes with selling it, and promoting it, and wheeling and dealing it, I don't like.

Q: *Is it difficult to be a woman in the industry?*

A: I remember being invited to Atlanta by a group called Women in Film. It was a feminist group and they wanted me to talk about women in film. I was very embarrassed because I don't believe in women's pictures. So I drafted them a speech. After my film, I warned them, I said "Listen, you've asked me to speak about women in film, and I don't believe in such a thing. I think people make films." I thought they were going to come crashing down on me because the audience was all women, and they were waiting to hear about women in film. There was a kind of stunned silence after I finished, and then they all started applauding. I said, "My goodness. Do you agree in principle?" And they said, "Yes. We think it's about time that kind of labeling in film was taken out." Ten years from now, I think this is all going to disappear. People are going to make films, women or men. I'm hoping that this will happen because I don't like being invited places that have a frame.

I'm always solicited to speak for women. I don't speak for crowds. I speak for myself. I don't like being melded into a mass, I never did. I think that a lot of pictures were made that were bad pictures, not because they were made by women, but because they were made by people who had no talent. They were made on the strength that women should make films. That played against women in films in a lot of ways. You should judge a script or a film on its ability alone, not necessarily on the gender of who does it, who writes it, or who plays in it. Women in film is a thing I've always had trouble accepting. You don't say men in films, gays in films, or blacks in films. People make films.

Q: *What about feminist films?*

A: Feminist films are another thing. I don't relate to that. It's something I don't know about. I suppose there's a use for it, but it doesn't concern me. I don't feel concerned by them.

Q: *If a woman has a flop her first time out, she'll often be excessively criticized, and find it difficult to make her next film. Do you find that to be true?*

A: Yes. I think that's par for the course. The first films by men are sometimes bad also, but they don't draw attention just because they're films by men. First films by women draw attention and they're particularly exposed if they're weak. Their weaknesses are less easily condoned because it's still a man's world. I think that the balance between who does what is starting to change. In Hollywood, it was strictly restricted ground up to five or six years ago. Now women are starting to work as professionals in the field, without being pointed out. I think it's gradually going to evolve, so that we no longer will be singled out. It's about time because it's an awful waste of energy to always have to deal with that. It's hard enough to work in pictures. In Hollywood there's a lot of decision-making by women. There was a point in Hollywood five years ago where almost a third of the studio VIPs were women. They were not giving contracts to women, they were working inside the industry as professionals, period.

Q: *What kind of pictures are you most interested in making?*

A: Mine. Not anybody else's. Mine. I still haven't found out exactly what kind of pictures I make. I know that I have ideas and I don't want them to be compacted into any kind of labels. They're my pictures. *Sonantine* was about two girls. *Handyman* was about a man. My next one is about a man. I have another that's only women. I don't cater to gender. A good story's a good story. I would like to speak more about what's in me than I would about social issues.

Q: *Are there any difficulties that you've experienced in your filmmaking that are specific to being a woman?*

A: I've never seen life through separate gender perspectives. I grew up not making the distinction. The only time that I really suffered as a woman was when I was an actress because there were no female parts. It was the only time I really thought of myself as a woman. When I worked in animation or when I worked in other places, it was never in my mind. I'm sure it was in my employers, but it was never a consideration in my mind. I was never stopped from doing anything because I was a woman. I drove bulldozers, and if I wanted to do something, I did it. I didn't stop because it wasn't done. The same is true when I started directing. It's only on the second film that I realized how much pressure a woman director can have from a crew. I remember once on set, it was an all male crew, and it was a particularly hard shoot on the subway because we had no control over the subway. I had to keep track of my staging, everything. At one point I was really tired of the guys chatting and making noises, because there was already enough noise in the subway.

So I said, and it was really a heartfelt cry, because we are able to express weaknesses that men don't, I said, "Come on guys, give me a break, I'm just a poor, helpless woman." They started laughing like crazy. I was so vexed. I thought, "I can't even say I need help, or I'm tired." I don't know what they thought, but they couldn't seem to imagine that I'd have any weaknesses as a director. I had to be above it all. That started me reflecting, thinking, "Oh, my God. The need to perform as a woman director is very, very strong. More so than a male director." And I was furious because they didn't give me the help I needed. They didn't stop talking and I had to work in this sound. I was in a really bad state then because I had just given birth. I shot three months after my first child was born. I was in terrible physical shape. I managed to do the film, but just. They had to carry me in the car every night because I collapsed. I fainted everywhere on the set. The guys used to have a running bet. That shocked me. They had running bets with the producer on whether I was going to finish the film. I don't think they meant it as a bad joke, but it struck me that they probably wouldn't have done that with a male director.

Q: *Doesn't that type of incident infuriate you?*

A: It doesn't anger me because I don't want to waste my time getting angry. I just went and got other people to work with, or tried to find better working conditions.

I'm certainly never going to make another film after I have a child. It was really foolish of me to do. I also want things to be very straight on the set. I don't want to have to sing for my supper, as they say, entertain the male crew. I don't necessarily believe in working with an all female crew, so I don't. I push it out of my mind. I think that its going to evolve as more women take to directing.

Q: *How has Quebec cinema, which is increasingly popular, evolved over the past few years?*

A: It's not Quebec cinema that has changed. It's just following its normal growth. It started twenty years ago as strictly documentary, and is now catching on to fiction. And drama is doing quite well. Quebec is learning drama, and is setting up the base for a dramatic film industry. But the public wasn't following. Now it's starting to follow. I haven't changed my way of making films, nor have others. It's the public that has changed their way of looking at them. What they wouldn't accept about themselves twenty years ago, they now do. They're ready to view themselves as fiction. They are ready to be invented. But I think that the essential change in Quebec has been with the public. The public looks at the films. Also the problem with generations. The people who went to films when several of us started were not educated spectators.

Now we're catching the younger audiences, that audio-visual generation that can look at images, and can relate to images. That makes an entire difference.

TEN

Deepa Mehta

Filmography

At 99: A Portrait of Louise Tandy Murch (1974), Short

K.Y.T.E.S.: How We Dream Ourselves (1985), Documentary

Travelling Light: The Photojournalism of Dilip Mehta (1986), CBC TV

Martha Ruth & Edie (1987), (co-director) Sunrise Films

Sam & Me (1990), Sunrise Films

The Young Indiana Jones Chronicles (1992), ABC TV

Camilla (1993), Miramax Release

Deepa Mehta is about to release her latest feature, the eleven million dollar *Camilla*. Reportedly the largest budget in Canadian film history to be handed to a woman director, the film stars Jessica Tandy and Bridget Fonda in the lead roles. Ironically, just a few years ago Mehta was struggling to find the financing to make her first feature, *Sam & Me*, based on a spirited, yet unlikely friendship between an aging Jewish man and a young East Indian who has just arrived in Canada. When she screened *Sam & Me* in Bombay, the audience was silent as the house lights went up. Mehta realized that they were used to seeing films that told the immigrant success story, not cinema that reflected immigrant reality. Mehta did not set out to make a sentimental cross cultural bonding story, but rather a story about prejudice — prejudice about age, class, color, and culture.

Her career as a writer, producer, director, and actor was established long before she started working in features. Born in Amritsar, India in 1950, she was exposed to film at an early age by her father who was a film distributor. After studying at the University of New Delhi and receiving a degree in philosophy, she started working on educational films and documentaries. In the early seventies she met Canadian filmmaker Paul Saltzman while they were both doing research in Delhi. They married and emigrated to Canada where she co-founded Sunrise Films with Saltzman and her brother Dilip Mehta, a successful photojournalist.

She has since produced over thirty television specials and directed an impressive string of films. One of Mehta's early award winning documentaries, *At 99: A Portrait of Louise Tandy Murch*, shows a healthy, active ninety-nine-year-old woman doing yoga, playing piano, and enjoying life. It works into one of Mehta's recurring themes, her belief that films should shatter rather than perpetuate myths. If that makes people squirm, she sees it as a confirmation of the message. As she says, "If people can see minorities as real human beings, complexities, flaws and all, then maybe we'll all be able to talk to each other."

$\mathbf{Q}$: *How did you develop an interest in film?*

A: My father was a film distributor in India. He owned a couple of movie houses. My exposure to film was watching what we call Bombay-B films. The Bombay film industry is one of the largest in the world and it's called Bollywood. They make these extravaganzas. Every film has about sixteen songs. It's really marvelous. There's usually this formula that most of them follow. They're about a man and a woman coming together, and then something happens to the man, he gets deathly ill or something, and the woman stands by him of course. Then they get married and one of them loses a leg or something and they get separated because an earthquake happens, or a famine, or a drought. They all get back together by the end and they sing a song. It's wonderful. I love them. So I started seeing them when I was very young, and I saw my first film called *Naugin* about forty times. It's about a woman who turns into a snake. Just what a seven-year-old needs, right?

Q: *Are these the kind of films that you thought you were going to grow up and make?*

A: I didn't think I was going to make films. I wanted to be a doctor. I wanted to save lives. All these people that I saw wounded and living miserable lives in India. I wanted to do something to help. So I wasn't thinking about making films when I was growing up.

Q: *So how did you end up becoming a filmmaker? Did that happen in India or after coming to Canada?*

A: I started making documentaries in India. I went to university in New Delhi, but I didn't study to become a doctor, I got my degree in philosophy instead. I stayed in Delhi and got a job at a film company that made documentaries. I was working with a group of really bright filmmakers. They were all Marxists, and I thought that was pretty interesting at the time. I started working with them as a typist and then they taught me to edit, and it sort of took off from there.

Q: *How did you come to Canada as a documentary filmmaker in the early seventies?*

A: I met Paul (Saltzman) in India. He had come to India to make a film on the High Commissioner, and I was researching the High Commissioner's daughter. So we met there, started going out, and got married. And it was my suggestion to leave India actually. I said to him, "Why don't we give Canada a try?" We came here and along with my brother Dilip [Mehta] we formed Sunrise Films.

Q: *How did* Sam & Me *come about, and what inspired you to make it?*

A: I had the idea for *Sam & Me*, and Ranjit [Chowdhry, the writer] had just moved here from India. I thought he was a wonderful writer. We talked about the idea and decided that he would write the script. We had no money. We were both flat broke, and of course we couldn't get any money from the agencies because Ranjit had just come here. But we somehow managed to do it anyway. We got it done. So after we finished, we had the first draft ready and the Executive Producer didn't like it. I couldn't believe it. Everybody was saying it wasn't ready, you should try this, you should try that. Maybe everybody was right. But I knew at that point that I had to make this film no matter what it took, that I would have a burning anger inside of me for the rest of my life if I didn't. It was very difficult to get it done. It was a labor of love. Passion. Pain. Some people call their films a labor of love, I call this one a labor of anger.

Q: *What prompted your move from documentary to drama?*

A: Nothing really prompted that move, it was a natural thing. I love documentaries, good documentaries. They can be so powerful. Film is really such a powerful thing. So coming from documentary and going into dramatic film, you learn about the power of script. You can actually control something. You can create it. You can shape it. You have nothing to lose. You can write whatever you want. You can make something that has the power to reflect what you think and what you feel. It just seemed the perfect thing to do, to go from documentaries into dramatic films, so that's exactly what I did.

Q: *Your films often reflect a sense of optimism within realism, for instance* Sam & Me, *and* At 99. *Is this a theme you've continued with* Camilla?

A: Absolutely. The reason that I really liked *Camilla* when I read it was that it struck a cord in me. Other scripts I'd read hadn't done that to me. *Camilla* had. It was a story about two women, one older and one younger. One who hasn't given up on life and one who has. It was the young one who'd given up. So yes, I'd been sent several scripts and when I read *Camilla* I knew that I wanted to do it.

Q: *How did you get involved with* Camilla?

A: Christina [Jennings, producer] sent me the script. She had already approached Jessica Tandy who was very interested in playing one of the lead roles. She had told Christina that if she ever got the project together, she would do it. Of course when you get a star like that, the budget increases. I think the budget ended up being about eleven million. Once you start getting big stars like Jessica Tandy or Bridget Fonda, everything goes up. The insurance for Jessica alone put the budget way up, I believe. And she gets script approval, director approval, things like that. But I didn't feel any pressure by that. There was complete confidence from Christina and Simon [Relph, producer]. You hear rumors of there being back up directors waiting to take over on these large budget films and things like that. But not once did they make me feel that there'd be someone standing there to take my job if I couldn't cut it. Not for a second.

Q: *Were you nervous working with a big star like Jessica Tandy?*

A: I was petrified. Are you kidding? And at first Jessica kept on saying, "Pardon me dear." And I thought that it must be my accent. I thought, "I've had it. I'm going to blow this because she can't understand a word I'm saying. It's going to be really intense." Then I discovered that she didn't have her hearing aid on. But yes, I was petrified. That goes away though. After about three days everything was fine.

One thing that I really think helped, something I've learned

Deepa Mehta on the set of *Camilla*

from previous films, is to get rehearsal time. I'm sure it's obvious and that everyone does it, but I insisted on at least three weeks rehearsal. I find it very useful. I rehearsed with Jessica, Bridget [Fonda], Maury [Chaykin], and Elias [Koteas]. We discussed the arc of the characters, where they were going and why. Then by the time we started filming, nobody was coming up to me and asking, what's my motivation, or anything like that. So I found that very good.

Q: *What was the jump like from a low budget independent film to an eleven million dollar picture?*

A: On the first day of shooting, I get out there and it's petrifying. It really is. The crew was so big. There were so many people. I'd never seen that many people on a film set before. The first couple of days were difficult, but again, once we started working together it was just so smooth. Everyone that I was working with was so great, it went along smoothly. So it wasn't such a big jump really, not a noticeable one. The craft service was very good [laughs]. That impressed me. I thought, "This must be the big time, because the craft service is good and I can get cappuccino on set."

Q: *Did it help that you had directed an episode of the* Young Indiana Jones *series between the two features?*

A: Doing *Young Indi* helped prepare me in ways that I didn't even realize. Just the scope of it, it being a Lucas production. It was invaluable working on that show, and working with him. But it was also overwhelming. I mean there I am at his company, at Skywalker, cutting with George Lucas. And it was also funny at times. The phone would ring and I'd pick it up. One time a man asked me if George was there. I asked who he was, and he told me it was Steven. I handed the phone to George and I asked, "Is that Steven Speilberg?" George said, "Yes it is," and he just sort of looked at me like I'd arrived from the moon. It was very funny. And even when George first called me about the job it was very comical. I remember he called and right off the top he said, "Hello, this is George Lucas." I thought it was some kind of joke, and I said, "Ha, ha, very funny," and I put the phone down. I hung up on him because I didn't believe that it was really him.

Q: *What has been the turning point of your career, the moment when you knew you'd arrived?*

A: Oh, I don't think I've arrived. But I guess the turning point was probably the reception of *Sam & Me* at Cannes. It was overwhelming. Just getting the film accepted there was a big point.

I thought that my film was going to die the typical Canadian film death at Famous Players, Cineplex, or the Carlton. So it was really a feeling of satisfaction. It didn't matter if I ever made another film again. That's what was so good. It was really wonderful to be able to complete something that meant so much, and to have it received in the spirit that it was made.

Q: *Do you think that your films are distinctly Canadian?*

A: Oh yes, I think they're really Canadian. They're idealistic. They're self deprecating. I think they have a lot of suppressed anger.

Q: *Do you think they reflect a woman's or East Indian's point of view?*

A: They must. I am what I am. I am a woman. I am an East Indian.

So my films must reflect that. Whether I'm making *Sam & Me,* which was a male cast, or *Camilla,* which is dominated by a female cast, I'll always bring my sensibilities with me. So I think that will always be there.

Q: *How have things changed for women, especially women in visible minorities in the past twenty years?*

A: I don't think it has. I really don't think it has. I think there are different problems. Things aren't any easier really. Maybe it will happen in the next ten years. Maybe it will change by the time my daughter grows up. But if you look at the number of women directing compared to men it's still so incredibly small. It's even the same for women working in Hollywood. I was reading an article in *Premiere Magazine* about Nora Ephron. She really had to fight to get the opportunity to direct *Sleepless in Seattle,* and she's a highly respected screenwriter, and she's directed Meryl Streep and Jack Nicholson. But she really had to fight for it. So I don't think things have changed that much at all.

Q: *Has anyone been influential in your career?*

A: There aren't really any directors. As a person who has influenced me I would have to say that it has been Louise Tandy Murch from my film *At 99.* One day we were filming her in these yoga positions. She had done this head stand about three times. And I asked her what had made her take up yoga at her age. She told me that when she turned ninety, she had thought to herself that she really should take up something different, and that she thought it would do her some good. She was so eloquent. So strong. She really turned my head around.

Q: *When you worked at Sunrise, you were more in the background. Since the success of* Sam & Me, *you have been in the foreground. How does that feel?*

A: I really don't think I am in the foreground. I don't feel like I'm socially in the film world at all. I've always been a pretty private person. This whole thing about if you do a film and suddenly everyone wants to talk to you — well if you do a flop who cares. It's a roll of the dice. So if you get caught up in that and start to think, "Oh well now I've arrived," then you're just setting yourself up. It's best not to get caught up in that.

Q: *What advice would you give to aspiring filmmakers?*

A: Well, I guess I'd say don't take yourself too seriously. Patience. You have to have patience. Passion. Persevere. You must persevere and persevere and persevere. I'm sure everybody says that and it means so little because it's just a word. It sounds so grandiose saying persevere, have passion, don't give up. It's so tough, how can you just say don't give up. At times you just say, "Is this worth it? Maybe I should just grow cabbages." What advice would I give? Nothing, probably nothing. You have to find it within yourself really.

ELEVEN

Mira
Nair

Filmography

Jama Masjid Street Journal (1979), Documentary

So Far from India (1983), Documentary

Children Of Desired Sex (1985), Documentary

India Cabaret (1986), Documentary

Salaam Bombay! (1988), Miabai Films Production

Mississippi Masala (1991), Samuel Goldwyn Release

The phenomenal response to Mira Nair's first feature, *Salaam Bombay!* in the Director's Fortnight at Cannes promptly changed the course of the thirty-one-year-old filmmaker's career. An uncompromising look at the lives of homeless children surviving the slums of inner Bombay, Nair's film won the Camera d'Or for best first feature, the Prix du Publique for most popular film at Cannes, and went on to receive an Academy Award nomination for best foreign language film. Nair's interest in exploring the lives of people who live on the fringe of society and her affinity for presenting filmic truth grew from years spent making documentaries. Turning her lens to fiction, she engaged Indian screenwriter Sooni Taraporevala to develop the script for *Salaam Bombay!*, recruited real-life street kids to play most of the roles, and shot the entire film in India using actual brothels and street locations. The authenticity that Nair captured by utilizing documentary techniques added significantly to the film's appeal.

Born in Bhubaneswar, India in 1957, Nair relocated to the United States when she was nineteen to attend Harvard University on a full scholarship. Initially interested in pursuing a career in theater, she found the study of traditional American musicals uninspiring and shifted her interest to documentary. She subsequently turned out four reality films that were shot primarily in India, and portrayed aspects of Indian life. *So Far from Home* is Nair's portrait of a young Indian man who immigrates to North America in search of a better life for himself and his family. But rather than living the big dream, he lands a lonely hotel existence in New York City and works as a low paid newsstand vendor. The prospect of moving his family fades as he adjusts to his new world and as he becomes increasingly unfamiliar with the life he left behind in India. Her final and most popular documentary, *Indian Cabaret*, serves up personal stories of strippers working in a Bombay nightclub, focusing on their strengths, resilience, and humor. To bring her second feature, *Mississippi Masala*, to the screen, she employed a full crew and a strong cast of actors that included Denzel Washington. Nair currently divides her time between America, where she carries on most of her work, Uganda, where she lives with husband Mahmood Mamdani and their son Zohran, and India, where she hopes someday to live again.

Q: Salaam Bombay!, *like many of your films, focuses on people living on the fringes of society. Why are you drawn to this type of material?*

A: I can see now in hindsight that that has become a theme of mine. I think it's because I'm drawn to the spirit of survival. You know when you just don't think you would have the guts to embrace a certain situation, you think you'd fall apart should it happen to you, and then when it happens you rise to the occasion. That type of resilience and courage in the face of adversity interests me, and also trying to make that kind of adversity have flamboyance or humor. That is inspiring to me. And I'm also drawn to it because it never takes on one language. It takes on many different expressions of the same struggle. It's universal.

Q: *What prompted your move from India to America, and sparked your interest in becoming a filmmaker?*

A: I was an actress in India, working on an amateur level in the theater there. When I was nineteen, I got a scholarship to study at Harvard. I planned to do my B.A. and pursue a career in the theater, but I wasn't very inspired because we were studying American musicals in the tradition of Oklahoma, and they didn't really have anything to do with me. So I stumbled into the next best thing, and at that college it was documentary filmmaking.

Right away I thought that it seemed to be a marriage of all my interests — of working visually, working with people, and capturing life. So for seven years I made documentary films, working very much in the cinema verité tradition. I shot them in India with themes very personal to me, and I would finish them in the West. Then I began to feel very impatient about waiting for things to happen. I wanted to control things more. I wanted to control the gestures, the nuances, and the light. I wanted to tell one's own story, but still very much from the point of view of capturing reality. That's what led me to make *Salaam Bombay!* in the way in which it was made. It was totally from life and about life, but it was completely set up.

Q: *You used real street kids in* Salaam Bombay! *How did you go about finding them, and how did you get them to be comfortable in front of the camera?*

A: I'd had the idea for the film since about 1983, but it was only in about 1986 that Sooni [Taraporevala, the screenwriter] and I went out to research it. We researched it much in the way that I would research a documentary, although I had no intention of making it a documentary. I was always sure that it would be fictionalized because, ironically, I felt that a fiction camera could get into these otherwise out of bounds spaces much, much better than a hidden camera could.

After researching, hanging out with street gangs, and writing our first draft — which was actually like a fourth draft for us — I rented a church in the middle of downtown Bombay. We put the word out that we were going to do a workshop. By that time we knew so many street kids that about one hundred and thirty of them showed up. We selected twenty four children and then we worked with them for seven weeks. We worked on a schedule, from nine to six daily, so that it would be like a job that they would have. I also invited my old theater directing friend Barry John, who I had worked with previously, to participate. We had this very unconventional workshop, showing them movies and videotaping scenes from our movie. The kids would refine scenes, and we would refine scenes. But basically we were trying to show them a way of acting without acting for the camera. At the end of the workshop they were ready to be in the film.

Q: *With a documentary background, and a somewhat experimental approach to your first feature, how were you able to raise the financing for* Salaam Bombay!?

A: It was murderous trying to get the money for it. I was raising money every day after shooting, getting money for the next day's shoot. It was really, really murderous. When we started it, I had never been to a fiction movie set before. I had one friend who made fiction movies and I got him to do a budget for me. It was out of sight. I believe the budget was about nine hundred thousand dollars. I was so depressed about it. I never could accept it really, because I thought it was impossible.

I thought I couldn't do it, that I couldn't raise that much. So what I did was make three budgets. I had my friend's budget, which was a comfortable budget in my opinion, then I had a basic 16mm budget, and I had a bare bones 16mm budget. I went to Channel Four in England, because they had given me ten thousand dollars to develop the screenplay. They decided that they would give me fifty percent of the film's budget. Based on that, I went to all kinds of places trying to raise the other money. I went to foundations and non-profit organizations in America. I tried to pre-sell the television rights to anybody who had bought my documentaries beforehand. But basically, nothing was coming through. I just had this offer on paper from Channel Four, but it wouldn't materialize if other money didn't materialize. And we had timed the whole shooting of the film around that massive festival which happens at the finale. So that meant we had to be shooting in the first week of September, when the festival happens. Therefore the workshop had to go on in June, July, and August; otherwise we wouldn't be ready.

So the workshop was carrying on because that was cheap. We could do that. But I was scrambling for money all during that time. One of the sources that I went to was the National Film Development Corporation in India which supports serious films, art films, whatever. They offered me what amounted to roughly one hundred and fifty thousand dollars. So I then presented the six hundred thousand dollar budget to Channel Four, saying that NFDC had given me one hundred and fifty thousand, that I had put in one fifty, which I hadn't because I didn't have it, and that therefore they should give me three hundred thousand. They agreed, and so I had in my hands four hundred and fifty thousand to make the movie.

I could have chosen right there to make the whole thing on 16mm, do it cheaply and suffer in distribution, or spend the whole wad on 35mm, make it decently, and suffer to get through post production. I made that film without any expectation or prediction of what would happen to it because it was so difficult just to make it, to keep making it, and to take it right to the finish line. Then two days after we finished it, we showed it in the Director's Fortnight at Cannes. It was one of those fairytale experiences where you go there a complete pauper and you somehow sell the whole world in twenty four hours. You don't know what happened or how. It's really a mind-blowing experience. Especially in hindsight, because you realize after that has happened just how difficult it is. It doesn't happen often. Then I spent nine months of my life doing what I consider the rape and pillage tour — which is the promotion of the film all over the world. It's good but not very enjoyable. It's very hard work, but mainly I was wanting to do another film.

Q: *Your next film was* Mississippi Masala. *Was it a big transition, going from the low budget experience of* Salaam Bombay! *to a Hollywood picture with a studio budget?*

A: No it wasn't. It seems to be big budget, but it isn't really. I was financed by people who had distributed *Salaam Bombay!* so I knew them. The fact that it had seventy-nine speaking roles and that we moved around to vastly different countries, it didn't mean that we had that much frill. It was made for six million dollars, and you have big stars.

It was made against a lot of adversity because at first everybody wanted me to do white things, and white issues. Many people were interested in me, but they were not interested in the film that I wanted to make. But, ultimately, *Mississippi Masala* was something that I wanted to do. It was completely my film throughout. I originated it, developed it, worked with Sooni [Taraporevala] as she did the script, all of that. So it was very much an independent film, both in spirit and in conception.

Q: *What inspired you about the story that drove you to make* Mississippi Masala?

A: The inspiration came from something that I had felt right from the time of being a student in America, of being a brown person in between black and white. I could move between these two worlds very comfortably because I was neither. So there's a sense of being accessible to both, but in a way belonging to neither. I perceived it as the hierarchy of color — of white, brown, and black. And then I read a newspaper article. I read it subliminally without any real plan of action. It was about the Asian expulsion from Uganda, which seemed to me like a time in history when this theme I'd been aware of had culminated and exploded. And that theme married into another theme that is prevalent to my thinking, and that's about what becomes home for people who settle, or are born already settled in other countries.

Mississippi Masala was a classic joining of these Indians who had never known India, who had made Africa their home, and had been thrown out because they were not black — other reasons too, but that reason on the surface — and of African Americans who had been born in America and had never known Africa. The movie explores these themes of home, and of displacement.

Q: *How did you develop the story, and write the script for* Mississippi Masala?

A: We developed the script from scratch. I heard about the Indians who owned motels in the Bible-belt of America, and first went there by myself. I was hanging out at various motels and I met quite a number of people. Then I went back with Sooni, my friend from *Salaam Bombay!*, and we started to develop a story-line together. We then went to Kampala, Uganda and Kenya, and we talked to a lot of people who had been thrown out. The script came out of that. There was six months of research and then the writing.

Q: *You've originated all your own films so far. Do you have any certain criteria in choosing your material?*

A: Whenever I get a script to read, or if there's a film that I want to make, I first look at it and wonder whether anybody else could do it. If the answer is yes, then I won't do it. It has to be very particular to me, and particular to me means something that gets under my skin. Not being from here, being from India and Africa, and all the other things that are part of me, they are all things that shape my world view. I come from a place of personal film-making. I make very personal films about things that are interesting to me. That's why I originate my own work. Although I'm open to reading scripts, and in fact the film I'm making right

Mira Nair on set with her son

now is from a script that was sent to me, still, it's most unusual for me to embrace something that I haven't developed.

Q: *Do you consider filmmaking to be a political tool for you?*

A: No. I have to make them provocative, so perhaps a political tool in that sense. My job is to provoke you into something, into re-examining something, or looking at something differently. I may provoke you into being shocked or being moved in some other way. Generally speaking, I don't get drawn to pieces of fluff. But film is not like an agenda or an instrument. I think that approach is generally reductive. I think the most exciting so-called political tools are those that catch up to you, that steal up from behind and make you think about something in an oblique way, rather than being direct.

Q: *How do you go about preparing the visual interpretation of a film?*

A: I have pretty eclectic influences. A lot of what I put into it comes from what I do between films, how I feed myself with certain cinema, energies or people, where I live, the paintings or photographs that I see, all of that. You don't just take a script, look at it, and start. It's a whole world of life that goes into it. It's about everything, even how I cook a meal, or how I dress my child. The movie I'm working on now is being done from a script that I received. It's about Cuban refugees who went to Miami in 1980 when Castro set the prisoners free. That's certainly not a topic that I've spent time thinking about in any direct way. So I've seen documentaries about it, read a lot about Cuba, looked at a number of photographic books, and gone to night clubs where Cuban music is played. Research is also an important part of it.

Q: *What qualities do you think a good director should possess?*

A: First and foremost I think that any director should not just simply direct films. A director should be a person who eats up the world. They should read, and write, and travel. I think they should be like a sponge — absorb things, put things out, communicate things. A director's world view should be a wide and varied one. You can't just read the trades and make references to the last film that you had on the screen. I find increasingly that it's the state of many directors in Los Angeles. So that's important, to have a broad education of the renaissance nature.

I also think that one should be very fierce about protecting one's own particularities. Don't smooth the rough edges of your own personality or interests. Develop them. Make yourself distinct from others in terms of how you think, and what makes your heart beat faster. Resist the common denominator.

And then there's this imperceptible thing which is just the power of making cinema. I don't know if people just have it or if they can learn it. I recently saw a film by a writer whom I really admire. It's his first film as a director, but it's just not a film. He doesn't understand that strange magic that must happen to make a story cinematic. That sense of cinema, of molding the actors completely, adjusting the pace of the *mise-en-scene*, and editing it in a way that is just smashing as opposed to flabby or sloppy. I can tell in less than ten minutes when I'm looking at a film whether the person has it or not. I cannot tell you what happens or how. It's just a cinematic magic that's either there or not.

Q: *Has anyone been inspirational to you, or had an influence on your career?*

A: Not as a mentor or anything like that. Sometimes I wish that there had been someone, because perhaps it would have been easier. I didn't have one path to follow such as an Indian woman role model whom I could look to. It's harder but it's also better in some ways. You get stronger because you don't have somebody whose footsteps you're following in, or whose door you're knocking on. Artistically, I find myself referring to the films of certain directors to keep me going. I watch Scorsese films. He fails many times, but even then I love him for taking the risks. I find myself studying him. Also Fellini, Kurasawa, Renoir, Buñuel, some of the older filmmakers. I find myself going back to the "classics" and really studying how they're put together. Things like that help me, but I don't have one person to tap into.

Q: *How have you been able to balance having a family with being a filmmaker, and living on the other side of the world when you're working in America?*

A: It's a funny thing, that saying about the other side of the world. There's this wonderful quote from Ferdinand Marcos, strangely enough. Somebody said to him, "But you live in the Far East." And he said, "Yes. Far from where?" If one thinks that L. A. is the center of the world, then I'm very far from it. But if one thinks that Kampala is the center of the world, I'm right in it. I'm one of those hybrids that has a foot in both worlds. It's funny because Kampala isn't even my world. I grew up in India. And I was heading back to India when I fell in love there and decided to have a baby.

I live very impulsively, but also Kampala is a very enchanted place. I love the land, I live with my husband there, and it's where our son is growing up. My son Zohran is not with me here. That's hard, really hard. He's with his father who is a professor of politics in Kampala. He will be joining me in two weeks, but I'll have been away from him for one and a half months. That's very painful.

Usually what I try to do is research or finish a screenplay when I'm in Africa, while I'm home and my husband Mahmood is working. And when I have to shoot, if I have to be away, I invite everybody in the family to join me. We create a big family wherever we are. It's what I'll be doing when I'm shooting in Miami. I'm going to rent a house and I've already been inviting family to come and stay. Therefore, when I go to work, Zohran will be surrounded by people he knows, and when I come home, I can have home cooked food and see my family. It's like carrying a caravan.

It's a little difficult with post-production, because I've shut up my home in New York. I'm only living in Kampala and very recently in New Delhi. That's tough, because technically they don't have post production facilities in either of those countries. I'll be in New York for five months doing the post on this film, and Mahmood is going to teach one semester at the University in New York, so we'll be together. Every movie is different. With each movie we try to work it out so that we can spend time together. But we've given ourselves until Zohran is five, and then we'll have to settle down and stay in one place more of the time.

Q: *Are there any final thoughts that you could pass along to aspiring filmmakers?*

A: The only thing that I would say is to have humility, have tenacity, and never give up. There's such a wave of young people directing, and I feel that sometimes it's mixed up with a kind of misplaced arrogance. That's what I mean about having humility — you have to submit yourself to learning in order to communicate what you've learned. You must have something to say.

TWELVE

Euzhane
Palcy

Filmography

La Messagere/The Message (1974), Short

L'Atelier Du Diable/ The Devil's Workshop (1981), Short

Sugar Cane Alley/Rue Cases Negres (1983), Orion Pictures

A Dry White Season (1989), MGM

In 1983 Euzhane Palcy, a twenty-five-year-old black woman from Martinique, the small French Island in the Caribbean, directed her first feature film, *Sugar Cane Alley*. Based on the novel *Rue Cases Negres* by Josef Zobel, the small independent film was made for less than one million dollars. The story focuses on life among the blacks of rural Martinique as seen through the eyes of a gifted young boy. Shot in black and white, it was a stunning feature debut for Palcy that gained her international acclaim and also caught the attention of Hollywood executives.

The offers that came from Hollywood were not of interest to Palcy, however, because they did not deal with black issues. Deciding to make a film about apartheid, she penned her own script based on a novel by Andre Brink. The script impressed producer Paula Weinstein who took the project to MGM and gave Palcy the opportunity to direct *A Dry White Season*. The tough political script also caught the attention of Marlon Brando who found the story so important that he decided to return to the screen after a lengthy break to join fellow actor Donald Sutherland in the nine million dollar feature. *A Dry White Season* gave Palcy the distinction of being the first black women to direct a major Hollywood feature film.

She was drawn to the idea of becoming a filmmaker when she was ten years old. Her goal was to give black people a voice, and to tear down the Hollywood stereotypes that many young black people are exposed to while growing up. Palcy is among the most controversial, political female filmmakers working today.

Q: *Coming from Martinique, a small French Island in the Caribbean, what attracted you to filmmaking?*

A: When I was ten years old, I decided to be a filmmaker because on the TV, and in theaters too, every time I had a chance to see a black actor in the movies and it was *always* an American movie, they had black parts, very stupid parts. I made a kind of wish. I said I have to be a filmmaker. I have to talk about my people. I have to show what black actors can play, and to give the real image of us, not stereotype us like that. The idea worked in my mind for many years. When I was fourteen years old, I found a book, a novel, *Sugar Cane Alley*. In French it's *Rue Cases Negre*. It was an event, because it was the first time in my life that I had a chance to have a novel in my hands written by a black writer and from my country. I said, "Oh my god, this will be my first movie. I have to make this because it's real, it's us." At the age of seventeen I started to write a first draft myself. I ordered books, cinema books from Paris, from a very well known cinema school to help educate me so I could write the first draft. I didn't want to go to Paris to study cinema, I just wanted to stay in Martinique and work at the television station. Many years later I decided to go to Paris and I made *Sugar Cane Alley*.

Q: *Why did you change your mind and decide to go to Paris?*

A: In Martinique it was difficult because, imagine you are a girl in Martinique, a young girl, and there is no cinema, only television. And you say, "Okay, I have to do it, I have to go to Paris to study and be the first filmmaker from Martinique to make movies." People tried to discourage me. They talked to my father and said, "Oh, how can you let your girl go to Paris, to France. It's very hard for people, the racism is very hard too. Aren't you afraid to let her go like that?" My father would say, "She is not a caprice, she really wants to do it, she has to be the first one. I have to help her." My father is a kind of feminist guy. He said okay. The only advice he gave me, the main one, was to study French literature, to have a chance to do something else just in case the filmmaking didn't work out. I followed his advice, and that's why my studies took ten years in Paris.

Q: *What kind of difficulties did you encounter in Paris?*

A: When I went to Paris, it was most difficult because I was a stranger. I had to fight, and I had to be the best. Not just good, but the best. I had to convince the French producers that this story, *Sugar Cane Alley*, was a universal story, and black people could play it.

Q: *How did you go about convincing them?*

A: To convince the French producers that I could make the movie was difficult. I was very young, I was black, and I was a woman. Three things that made it very hard for them. Also, I had a story with just black roles, no stars, no French actors, nothing. I fought for two years and eventually I found a wonderful producer who had helped many women in film to make their first movie. He said, "Oh I love that story. I really believe in that story. I will help you to make the movie." Thanks to him it is a movie.

There was so much opposition, even about the grandmother character. The actress had played in a hundred and fifty movies with big stars. And in all of them she had a small part, what we call a black part, a servant, a nanny. She never got to play more than that. For the first time in her life, at seventy-six years old, she got a real part. A chance to show people how good she is. In various festivals she got the prize for best actress. I was happy for her, but I was also sad, and I cried, because I realized that it was a wonderful gift for her, but it's her first one and her last one because she is old now. We need to be 10 or 7 filmmakers, black filmmakers all over the world, to write for our actors and our actresses. People who have the finances, or power to decide about movies should be more open-minded and not call an actress just because she's a black actress, or an Arabic actress or Spanish. They should say, "Oh this women is great. She is talented. Even if she's black she can play this part." They should do that more often.

Being black filmmakers, we need to write stories for our people, and give them a chance to act too. I realized that's why I was very angry when I was a little girl and I said I have to be a filmmaker. I chose this job not for the money, because you must be crazy when you are doing this kind of job to think you'll make money. I just love it. I just love it because to me it's a very difficult choice, and it's a very important choice for people, for women, for blacks, you know. All of that is very important.

Q: *What happened after* Sugar Cane Alley *came out?*

A: *Sugar Cane Alley* was very successful all over the world. We got forty international prizes for this movie, and that was a very big event for me. It changed my whole life. But inside I will never change myself. I will always stay the same Euzhane that people know. When people in Hollywood saw the movie, they called me. Warner Brothers called me and proposed for me to work with them. I said, "Okay, but I already have a project, and if you want to work together, you should have a look at it." They did, and they just loved the subject. They said, "Okay let's do it." I've spent three and a half years working on the same project since *Sugar Cane Alley*. I've refused other projects because I'm focusing on this one. I chose it, and I know that I cannot veer from it. I'm very different. Maybe because I'm from Europe. I cannot make a movie if I cannot feel the story. I chose to be a filmmaker, not to make money or commercial movies. I want to love the story.

My producer accepted to work on this story, and we are still working on it. I just decided to do the writing myself, because after six drafts I was so disappointed. I was sad because no screenwriter could write the story with the same feelings, the same passions that I felt. I was sad about that. I said, "Okay, I can forget that I lost three years, but only if I write the story myself, and I make the movie." They accepted, and let me write the story.

Q: *What are your feelings about filmmaking in the Third World?*

A: In Africa there are few. We cannot say there are many filmmakers, because the first problem is lack of money for production. They are trying now to organize themselves, to establish a cinema structured for production. In the Caribbean there are many young girls and boys who are dying to study film, dying to make movies, and they are trying all the time to do it, with the 8-mm cameras. They make short movies. In the Third World, people grow up with the song, the light and the colors and the

Euzhane Palcy directing a scene from *Sugar Cane Alley*

music. It's very important for them to try to express that, but the main problem is a problem of money. Festivals might change that. In Martinique, for example, in June every year, we've had a special festival, not just for cinema but for visual arts in general. *Sugar Cane Alley* opened a big door for Third World filmmakers. For example, before, when people from my country or from Africa used to bring their scripts to producers, as soon as they turned their backs the producer put the story in the garbage, because they didn't care about it. They just didn't want to read it.

But now with the success of *Sugar Cane Alley*, producers are hungry. They want subjects about the Third World. They want subjects about black people. They are interested. Now in France we have five movies with black people. Since *Sugar Cane Alley* was a success, they know that there is an audience for this kind of movie, and that people want to know more about the Third World. That's very encouraging for us as Third World filmmakers.

Q: *Are there many women directing films in France?*

A: They are so numerous. When I studied cinema, there were few women in the school. I got my degrees and I left. Now in every course, they have more girls than boys. And that's just great. I'm happy. For example, with my next movie, I will be so happy to have women around me. I'm not sexist, but I just love it. We have women for the lighting, women cameramen, and we have to work together. That's good. I was talking with a friend and I said, "Look, I'm not trying to say that because we are women, we're the best, it's not that. But every movie made by a woman is different, of course, because women are different from men."

Q: *Is it difficult making a film in Hollywood?*

A: The production here in Hollywood is quite different than in Paris and Europe. Everybody knows that. When a producer in Hollywood calls a French filmmaker, a European filmmaker, to work here, we are happy. It's good for us. At the same time, we are very anxious because in Hollywood there are no producers in a hurry, just filmmakers in a hurry. Filmmakers are in a hurry to make their movie, but for the producers three years is nothing. When they told me that I was so shocked. I said, "Oh my God, I don't want to wait three years." But if we make the movie as good as we can, I can forget those three years. I can say, okay we have a good movie.

Paula Weinstein was my executive producer on *A Dry White Season*, and I'm so happy to work with her because she is just great. She is smart and she knows exactly how to deal with the script. It's very difficult to find people who can speak the same language as you, and I found that with her. Once we spent a week working on the script, to make cuts because my script was too long. During that week, sometimes at seven in the morning, she'd call. "Euzhane, I cannot sleep because I'm worried about this and that." We'd discuss it and I'd think maybe you are right. Every time she was like that. We were like two pregnant women waiting for the baby. It was so great. I just love it, and I love to work with her. Also, she's very political and she understood the subject. We spoke the same language, and she had the same passion that I had for *A Dry White Season*. Even when I said I would write the story myself, she said, "Oh great, you should do it." She encouraged me to do it.

THIRTEEN

Lea Pool

Filmography

Un Strass Café (1979), NFB Documentary

La Femme de L' Hotel (1984), Association Co-operative de Production Audio Visuals

Anne Trister (1986), Cine 360 Inc.

A Corps Perdu (1988), Telescene Films Montreal and Xanadu Films Zurich

Hotel Chronicles (1990), NFB Documentary

La Demoiselle Sauvage (1991), Aska Film Distribution

Montréal Vu Par (1991), Short within a Feature, Atlantis Releasing

Lea Pool, born in Geneva, Switzerland, is known internationally as one of Canada's most prominent female directors. After graduating from the University of Quebec with a degree in communications, Pool made dramas, documentaries, and variety programs for Radio Québec. Her first film, *Un Strass Café*, was a short documentary made at the National Film Board of Canada. Her stunning feature film debut, *La Femme de L'Hotel*, won both the Critics' Prize and the International Critics' Prize at the Montreal World Film Festival, as well as Best Canadian Film at the Toronto Festival of Festivals. The story is set in a downtown Montreal hotel and focuses on a female director who encounters a woman who is heartbroken from a previous love affair. While *La Femme* hinted at lesbianism, the subject was brought to the forefront in Pool's next film, *Anne Trister*. A loosely autobiographical story of a young Swiss immigrant who falls in love with an older woman, the film created a stir at the prestigious Berlin Film Festival and gained critical acclaim in Canada. Although the film deals with homosexual themes which are often hard to market, *Anne Trister* was a commercial success, playing in Montreal theaters for almost six months.

Her third feature, *A Corps Perdu*, is the story of Pierre, who returns home to find his two roommates gone. Alone with the cat and some photographs, Pierre proceeds to start documenting the fragments of his identity and his relationships. The film won first prize at both the Namur and Atlantic Film Festivals. *Hotel Chronicles*, produced for the series Parter D' Amerique, questions the great American myths. From a hotel in New York to a Navajo reservation, Pool explores these myths with documentary footage and letters. *La Demoiselle Sauvage* is based on a short story of the same name by Swiss author Corinna Bille. Shot over three seasons, the exteriors were all done at various times in the Grimentz area near the village of Chandolin in Switzerland, and all of the interiors were shot in a Montreal film studio. The film tells the tale of Marianne (Patricia Tulasne) who flees to isolation in the mountains after a violent attack. Elysees (Matthias Habich) discovers her after she collapses at the foot of a dam, and they fall in love, only to be torn by fear, commitment, and betrayal.

Lea Pool's latest film is *Rispondetimi* for *Montréal Vu Par*.

Q: *Could you tell me about* La Femme de L'Hotel, *the main theme?*

A: *La Femme de L'Hotel* is about a lot of things, but what was most important for me to speak about was three sides of a woman. It was very difficult to relate those sides with only one woman, so I chose three different women. Each one is a side of me in a way. For example, the character of the filmmaker is the one who creates, and she is also the intellectual, conscious side of a woman. The silent woman who comes into the hotel, *La Femme de L'Hotel*, is the stranger, the person we don't know anything about. She is the unconscious part of a woman. And between these two women, there is the actress. She is the one between the conscious and the unconscious part of a woman. It's also a film about exile, the exile from one country to another, because the filmmaker has come back to Montreal after eight years. And also the exile of a woman, how you feel inside and outside. The outside for me is more the city, the urban part of the film, the inside is the hotel. And finally, it is a film, as *Anne Trister* is, about love and creation. The filmmaker cannot create without the love of the femme de l'hotel, but its an impossible love, something she cannot reach.

I think if she could reach this love, she'd have no necessity to create any more. She needs this impossible love to create. These are the main purposes of the film.

Q: *Do you feel you have a responsibility to create on screen images of women?*

A: I am a woman, and what I am interested in is the image of a woman. I think we have very few films that speak of women, and are from the point of view of a woman. This for me is important. I don't know if I will always do that type of film, but right now it is very important for me, and perhaps the most important reason to make films.

Q: *You've been compared to Von Trotta in your work; do you see any similarities?*

A: Yes, a little. I like the films of Margarethe Von Trotta. For the

German version of *Anne Trister*, Margarethe Von Trotta did the translation. What is similar I suppose is the friendship between women, and the situation of men in front of women. This I think is very close, but I think that our style is different. We don't tell stories the same way.

Q: *What is unique about Quebec cinema?*

A: It is difficult for me to answer that question, because I think my films are a little bit apart from most Quebec films. That's what I was told anyway. There are very different kinds of Quebec films, and I cannot put one word to it. I hate all the distinct categories about what is a Quebec film, what is a German film, or what is a woman's film, because I don't think it's ever so separate. I know a lot of woman filmmakers, that in my opinion don't make women's films. I know also some women filmmakers who do make women's films. In Quebec, I couldn't tell you who is really a Quebec filmmaker. But I think for two years now, there has been something interesting happening in Quebec. I don't know what it is exactly, but I think we have developed a stronger international market. *Le Decline de L'Empire American, Un Zoo la Nuit,* and *Anne Trister* are three different films for me. There's nothing to compare, and they are three Quebec films.

Q: *What about the fact that Quebec cinema has been compared to European cinema, whereas films from English Canada are said to be cheap Hollywood imitations?*

A: I think that there are two categories of filmmakers. I think there are filmmakers whose biggest desire is to go to Hollywood. Then there are other directors who are closer to European cinema, and perhaps not as concerned with commercial success. They're more film d'auteur. I think especially these past two years we're seeing the distinction between these two kinds of films. I know for example that my films are better received in Europe than in English Canada or the United States. I think it's because of the theme, because of the style, because of what I am telling. I don't make films that have a lot of chance in Hollywood.

Q: *Could you tell me about the effect* La Femme de L'Hotel *had on your career?*

A: Yes. The first time that *Femme de L'Hotel* was shown was in the Montreal Film Festival. It was very interesting for me because it was met with a very good reception, and we won the International Critics' Prize. Just after that, we went to the Toronto Film Festival and there we won the CITY TV prize for Best Canadian Film. And after that, there were many other prizes, in Chicago, and in Paris at the Festival des Films des Femmes. It was also nominated for a Cesar in Paris and for two Genie Awards in Canada, one for the music, and the other for Louise Marlot as Best Actress. So it was very important for me because it permitted me to write a new film, and to raise the money quickly, so I could make *Anne Trister* at the National Film Board soon after.

Q: *Do you feel you have to compromise your films in order to get financing?*

A: It's difficult to say. For example, my first film was *Strasse Café.* It was a sixty minute film. I made it all alone. I was the producer, I was the director, I was the editor, I was the screenwriter. And I showed the film only when it was completely finished, so I knew that this film was completely me. When you begin to work with money you have to show your script to different societies — Telefilm Canada, Societé Général de Cinema Québécois, the National Film Board — and there are always people who read the script and say, "Oh, I don't like this," or "I prefer this." Of course you try to keep in mind exactly what you want to do, but you also change little things here and there. And in the end, you're never sure if it was exactly what you wanted to do.

Q: *In* Anne Trister, *the love scene between Anne and Pierre is graphic. The love between the two women is much more suggestive. Is this a conscious choice?*

A: Yes. It's very different because the subject is very different. In that film, the question is the beginning of love, the desire. I try to show the desire between two people. Since these two women are with men at the beginning, I think it's normal that I show the

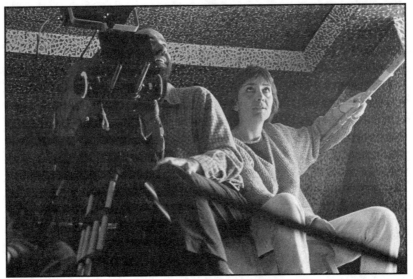

Lea Pool directing a scene from
Anne Trister

love scene with men as something normal, because it was normal for them. What happened between these two women was something very new for them. I wanted to show it with much more discretion. It's not a question of censorship, not at all. I think that in the way their eyes look at each other I show much more than in the first love scene between Pierre and Anne. Because something is happening that you can't really see. One love scene between two women that I find very beautiful, but very difficult, is in the Chantel Ackerman film *Je Tu Il Elle*. She plays herself, and the camera is fixed, and I think the scene is twenty minutes long. I don't know exactly. And the light is very strong, and it's a very realistic scene. In my films I try to show this more with the emotion, with the eyes, with the gestures. I think for this film it would have been an error to show it differently, because this film is much more about creation than love. The same in *La Femme de L'Hotel*. If it becomes too realistic, I think all the artifices crash. I think it's very important to keep the emotion completely there, but not to fulfill the desire. Because I think the creation is something that is not fulfilled.

Q: Anne Trister *and* La Femme de L'Hotel *both have themes of a woman loving another woman running through them. Is this a theme you are particularly interested in exploring?*

A: I think this is a preoccupation of women at large. I think not only lesbian women, but all women have this kind of preoccupation. Every woman is born from a woman, the first contact, the first relationship, the first love, all these things are with another woman. If you don't speak of a woman loving another woman, you might speak of a woman loving a mother. In *Anne Trister*, it's not very clear but it's also a question of mother love. I think every woman who is looking at this does so because we lost this when we were young. With a man we can never find this again, so it's normal that we are preoccupied with this.

Q: *How did you become a filmmaker?*

A: I never chose to be a filmmaker. I was a teacher in Switzerland and I wanted to introduce video to the students in my class. There was nowhere to learn how to make films and video in Switzerland at that time, so I came to Montreal. They had a special program at the university, so I went there for one year, and stayed for the beginning of the second year. In the second year you had the chance to make a little film and people found my film interesting. It was a documentary film about a porter of a big hotel. I very often have hotels in my films. So it began like this, but I never chose to make films.

Q: *Are there any female filmmakers whose work you admire?*

A: I think the most important for me is Chantel Ackerman. She's a friend also. I knew her before I made films, so I was very interested in what she was doing. Perhaps it's she who gave me the strength to make films.

Q: *What is the most important thing that you are striving for as a filmmaker?*

A: I think what is the most important, what I want to see the most, is something that is honest. I see too many films that are money films, that are commercial films. They're from the point of view that you put together all these different ingredients and hope that the salad will be good. It's very rare to see films now that come from the heart. It can be different kinds of films. I like comedies, I like dramas, and I like a lot of films. If I feel that a person really has to say something, that it's so important that if they don't say it they will die — to me that's a good film.

FOURTEEN

Patricia Rozema

Filmography

Passion: A Letter in 16mm (1985), Short, CFMDC

I've Heard the Mermaids Singing (1987), VOS Productions

White Room (1990), VOS, for Alliance Releasing

Montréal Vu Par (1992), Short within a Feature, Atlantis Releasing

In 1987, Patricia Rozema unveiled her first feature film, *I've Heard the Mermaids Singing*. The quirky little offbeat comedy was an instant hit, earning the then twenty-nine-year-old Canadian director international recognition as well as immediate star status on her home turf. Rozema set out to make a movie in which people would respect a woman they wouldn't normally pay attention to, and show her as heroic rather than pitiful, even though she was an underdog. The combination struck an emotional cord in people. At the core of *Mermaids'* sweeping appeal is Polly, the film's charismatic heroine. A naive, awkwardly shy, and "organizationally impaired" girl Friday, Polly also possesses talent as a photographer, an activity that enables her to live out a rich, eccentric fantasy life, and eventually helps lift her above the superficial hypocrisy of her work at a chic art gallery, and her obsessive attraction to the gallery's curator (played by Paule Baillargeon). Rozema set the stage for the phenomenal reaction to *Mermaids* by writing, directing, editing, and co-producing, then Canadian actress Sheila McCarthy assured Polly's loveability by playing the lead role to charming perfection. Rozema has cast McCarthy in both her subsequent films.

Born in 1958, Rozema was raised in a Dutch immigrant family in Southern Ontario before going to Michigan to get her B.A. in Philosophy and English. With an award-winning short to her credit, some experience in journalism, and a few stints as second or third assistant director on Canadian features for David Cronenberg and Don Owen, Rozema raised $350,000 to make *Mermaids*. Her main source of creative support came from Canadian co-producer Alexandra Raffe, who teamed up with her to form VOS Productions. In 1990 Rozema and Raffe released their second feature, *White Room*. While the film was accomplished, many critics were less enthusiastic in their response. She followed *White Room* with a segment in *Montreal Sextet*, a feature in which six of Canada's most prominent directors pay tribute to Montreal's 350th birthday with short, cinematic interpretations of the city. Recently, Raffe and Rozema decided to part ways, at least for now.

Q : *What was that moment like in your life when you went from being unknown to having worldwide fame, and with hindsight how do you feel about all that success?*

A: *I've Heard the Mermaids Singing* was invited to the Directors' Fortnight in Cannes. We thought, "Is that good? What is the Directors' Fortnight?" So there was a lot of research about the different categories in Cannes. As the research came in we discovered that this was the best place in the whole wide world for this film to be screened for the first time. I felt very much like a person who had done well in kindergarten and was now being invited to lecture at a university hall. I anticipated a career of tiny little advancements, and then suddenly this happened. After the screening in Cannes I was shocked. It was thrilling to walk down those steps and see all of those people. I didn't have much to compare it to, and later I found out that it was a sort of minor miracle. It doesn't happen all the time. I'd only had one film and I'd only been to Cannes once. I had no idea how to put that experience up against some kind of constant. So walking down the stairs there really moved me, and actually made me feel understood. Then distributors started coming up to me and quoting their box office on other films. I didn't care if this film made a million here, and that film was into overages already. I didn't care. I wanted to talk about that later.

Then I went out for dinner with some members of the press and I asked somebody to tell me honestly what the weaknesses were in my film. He told me, and I went into the bathroom and I cried my heart out. I thought, "Rozema you're really becoming neurotic." But I realized that I would be up for that kind of thing all of my life. I could not come out of the blue again. I could not work privately, I could not have failures quietly. I would always be free game. I was a good, legitimate target for any kind of criticism. Because once you've reached that level of fame, the next film would be up for that kind of criticism. That was really sad for me at that time. I should have just laughed and danced the night away, but I got really complicated about it.

Q: *Do you regret that sudden success?*

A: Little increments would be fun, but then you hit your stride when you're forty-five, and it's fun to be floating around the world when you're twenty-eight. Lots of people make a pretty good first film, but somehow the timing isn't right, the placement isn't right, the mood isn't right, or the collective unconscious isn't quite right. It doesn't take off, and you don't necessarily get to make your next film for another two, three, or four years. You lose a kind of emotional energy. So in that respect I'm more than happy.

But it's like first love. There's a big, big romance where you realize you're allowed to be a filmmaker. I could legitimately, and without arrogance, put "filmmaker" on my passport and it was okay. That moment is exciting, and it's a loss of virginity in a way because every moment after that, filmmaking is just your job. It's what you do. There will never be the same kind of excitement about what you do — not for yourself, and not for others. Never quite the same excitement.

Q: *Tell me a bit about your background and how you got into film.*

A: I got out of school with a degree in English and philosophy and a minor in journalism. I did some internship work in Chicago and New York on various television programs. *The Journal* (on CBC TV) was just starting up so I bombarded them with phone calls and information about myself. It's kind of obnoxious really, but I have no shame if I want something. I called them a lot, had an interview, the interview went well and I got the job. Eventually I found out that it really wasn't my element in a way, because I'm not a Current Affairs junkie with an encyclopedic knowledge of contemporary life, which I think is the ideal journalistic mind. I was constantly frustrated that I couldn't mold the stories more. Then the CBC had cutbacks and they fired me. I was absolutely alarmed that I was getting fired because I'd always done well in things. It really pulled the rug out from under me. I was completely shocked. So I decided to go on UIC [unemployment insurance] and do a film.

Q: *What inspired you to make* I've Heard the Mermaids Singing?

A: I think every film is a reaction to the last film. I'd made a half hour about a successful career woman and the first thought I remember having was, "I feel like doing a film about an unsuccessful career woman." I was seeing so many images of powerful women around and I thought that it was as oppressive as only seeing images of weak women. So I wanted to focus the story on an unsuccessful career woman, someone who doesn't really deserve a lot of attention. Essentially I just wanted someone who was artistically unsophisticated. I also wanted to make the point to anyone who wanted to listen that art-making is not about being excellent, it's about doing what you have to do. If you absolutely need to do it, you'll probably be neurotic if you don't, so just do it and fuck them if they don't get it.

Q: *Do you think of yourself as a political filmmaker?*

A: No. I'm not really. I'm quite feminist by nature. I grew up in a fairly feminist household. My father has always loved really strong women, and my mother was one. The whole family had a respect for these sort of noble, vocal women and their opinion mattered very, very much. I see myself much more as an artist, and I think that a political agenda sometimes interferes with art-making. It's not the highest thing on my agenda. I don't know if I'm proud of that or embarrassed by that, but it's just not my automatic tendency.

Q: *If it's not a political tool for you, what do you want people to walk away from your films with?*

A: Ultimately, the best thing would be that people felt for people they've never felt for before. I think that's the highest purpose that fiction can serve, is to create empathy in a place that you've never felt empathy before. To slip inside the soul of the most unlikely person is something that fiction can do in a way that almost nothing else can. Documentary can do that, but I've got a fictive turn of mind, I guess. So that's what I would like. I would like them to walk away with understanding. When you start out you don't know what your thing is, what your focus is, or your issues are. As you go along you figure out, "Yes, I keep veering back to this, I keep veering back to that." And I'm just starting to realize that I veer naturally towards anything that's absurd and sad. If I can put those two things together in a scene, I think it's a good scene.

Q: *What did you want to say when you made* White Room?

A: The story is seen through the eyes of Norm. I really like inarticulate characters, people who just don't have words for what they feel. That really moves me — the idea that people feel a huge, huge expanse of feelings and they just don't have the means to get it out there. They can't get it out on paper because they never learned to write very well. They can't get it on film because they're not a filmmaker. I believe that just about everyone is a frustrated artist in some way. I think that's why *Mermaids* worked, because it showed respect for someone who wasn't getting respect artistically. *White Room* was a next step from that. *White Room* is this weird ambiguity or weird thing that happens. If you're really honest and make art that really touches people, then you have to protect yourself. It's why sunglasses are so associated with stardom, because it's through their eyes that we feel contact with these actors. That's where all of the intimacy and all of the energy is and that's what they have to protect in the end. So it's the thing that's the most intimate that has to be protected. That's what *White Room* was about.

Q: *Did the success of* Mermaids *make* White Room *harder or easier for you to make?*

A: Definitely harder. I think success almost always makes the next thing financially easier and artistically harder. Tennesee Williams wrote a beautiful, beautiful essay on that bitch success. You need limitations artistically to create something that has integrity. I don't think that you need financial limitations, but you have to be very, very sure of yourself. I think I was, and I'm really pleased with what I did. I know that I could only do that after a big success because there's some bite in it. There's some really tough, sharp edges, and people that you are drawn towards who suddenly turn twisted. It had a jagged nature to it, tied up in a fairy tale.

Q: *The media embraced you as a darling in the film world when you released* Mermaids. *Was there pressure to live up to what they'd started?*

A: Let's put that in perspective. I was a media pimple compared to just about everyone else. But in Canada's little filmmaking world, yes, there was some pressure on me and some awareness of what I was about to do. I think the complication in that is second guessing yourself instead of just going for your gut taste in things.

You end up saying, "I like that. Do I? I've already done that. I'm imitating myself already. I've got to stretch. But if I stretch too much then I'm off my sure ground." So you've got far too many voices in your head, far too many voices. The hardest thing in film is to speak with one pure, strong voice right from beginning to end. To have one clear tone, one pace that's coherent, one story that's told as if it was just made up at that moment, that's what you want to do. So if you've got a million voices, others as well as your own, then it's far too complex a situation. You can end up ordering a pizza with too many ingredients on it.

Q: Mermaids *cost $350,000. Did the low budget create limitations on what you wanted to do, or on the contrary, did it give you a sense of creative freedom?*

A: Have you ever had $350,000 in the bank? It's an extraordinary amount of money for an individual to have to indulge their little fantasy. I was overwhelmed to think that I would be given that kind of trust. It's way too much money for something that's pure pleasure. So I didn't consider it a handicap at the time, not at all.

Q: *You hadn't directed a feature before* Mermaids. *How were you able to raise the money?*

A: *Passion* showed a technical competence which is one of the big fears for people with money. So, I could show them technical competence. I could show them Alex Raffe [the producer] who is extraordinarily organized and looks like she's much more serious and stable than I might be. And I could show them a script that moved people. A big discovery for me was seeing that the lines people liked in the script were the lines people liked in the film. I put a lot of weight on the script. I'm very much a writer/director and I see both roles as important. I have learned from my two shorts and two features to take the script stage seriously, because that's when it's easy to change things. You can't think that things will change when you get the actress, when the sound is done, or when you get the music. It doesn't change from it's basic initial inspiration — and that is the story on the page.

**Patricia Rozema on the set of
Montréal Vu Par**

Q: *As a writer/director, how are you able to make each film different than the ones preceding it?*

A: It's an extraordinarily disorganized, amorphous process, and I'm very afraid of getting my thing down. I think artists are pushed into that very quickly. People are quick to say, "You do the road movie tough guy biker thing, you do the disenchanted youth urban thing, or you do the whimsical happy-go-lucky isn't life sweet and sad thing."

You will be typed very, very quickly because there's so much press in the world. There's so many voices and arms of the press, it's like walking into mirrors a lot. You end up looking at yourself way more than you need to.

Q: *How do you work out the visual attitude of a film with the cinematographer? How do you interpret the film once you've written it?*

A: We'll watch movies together. The framing and composition is my job. I take suggestions every which way, but ultimately that's just me. With lighting I have to trust some more. I make decisions long before we shoot and try to find a few words for the tone, a few for the theme, and a few for the camera style. That way when we're sitting there and we don't have time, I can always fall back on those few words. I can say, "Oh yes, choppy and blunt," or," I remember it was going to be fluid and mostly from above."

Q: *Are there any directors who have inspired your career?*

A: No director inspired my career. I think some filmmakers are influenced by seeing certain films, and others pick film because it happens to be the current popular art form. I think I'm one of those. I wasn't so in love with cinema from an early age that I couldn't resist. I was in love with music, business, pictures, acting, and stories. I think you have to have something to prove, because otherwise you don't have the energy for it. If you're asking about directors that I like, Jane Campion seems like a goddess to me. Really thoughtful, very artistic. Profound and amusing. I never used to list any women filmmakers. I wasn't going to pick women's films just because they were women. I think that's the greatest injustice. But then when Jane Campion came on the scene, I remember feeling hugely affirmed by it and thinking, "Yes, yes, and it's a woman." She's an elegant filmmaker. I haven't seen one false move on her part. Every step has been sure. There's lots I love about Mike Leigh — *High Hopes, Life Is Sweet.* His films have completely naturalistic acting. Truffeaut has such a gentleness and kindness in his work, so much warmth in his characters. I fell asleep in *Star Wars.* I can't stay awake in action adventures, or where people are running after money or after bad guys, or being chased by bad guys. I need some kind of psychological twist. Action isn't enough for me. It's not what draws me. Sally Potter's film *Orlando* has an aesthetic. It's expansive and lush, and still ironic and intellectually rigorous. It's stylized, but respectful of story, respectful of narrative. I think that narrative is the way to keep people with you.

Q: *Do you find anything distinctly Canadian or feminist about your films?*

A: Canadian, yes. It's the underdog thing I guess. That's what they all say. I just do my own little obsessions and I guess I reflect where I come from. When I was writing the proposal for *Mermaids,* I saw

Polly representing any underdog in Canada. She's politically, eco-nomically, and somehow ego-wise an underdog internationally. I was raised in Canada, but I went to school in the States. When I came back to Canada I was shocked at how timid people were, how they just didn't dare to look you in the eye and ask you what they wanted. I was really shocked and unnerved by it. I'd spent five or six years in the States where everyone mouths off, so I came off more aggressive than I actually felt. The image that people fed back to me of myself was of someone quite aggressive, and I thought I was actually very timid. So that might have inspired Polly, someone that fragile. Norm has a great deal of Canadian traits in him. And the role of Jane, played by Kate Nelligan, that's a real classic Canadian character — the person who has much to offer and yet doesn't dare to say it. I think we have a whole history of artists like that in this country.

Q: *Is there anything distinctly feminist about your films?*

A: I'm distinctly feminist. My films assume feminism. That's the best way I can say it. They assume feminism, it's in their founda-tion. All of the assumptions of the characters and everything that happens assumes that women clearly have the right to do what-ever they want to do — clearly have the right to own property, to run the world, whatever. I'm very, very much a feminist. I believe that women have been held back unnaturally and unjustly. It's tragic what the world has lost. I think there's this testosterone dis-ease that has made boys kind of trample over girls for too many centuries, especially in centuries where muscle matters. Now we're getting to a state in the world where brawn is not nearly as necessary, and consequently you have the skills of women being recognized a bit more readily. I think that it's quite horrid that women have been held down and held back. But I believe that history does progress and that we are somehow recognizing the stupidity of that.

Q: *Can you tell me about your collaboration with Alex Raffe, and a bit about your future plans?*

A: We have worked together quite well. She has a business back-ground. I don't have business training or anything, not even an inclination toward it. So that was a great complimentary set of skills for us. She's a good reader, and has a high standard for story, for psychological truth and for originality.

We had quite a smooth collaboration because our skills were so completely different, and our types of intelligence were so completely different. Mine is to step back, step back, step back, to pretend I'm on another planet, to see it from as great a distance, and see it in it's most simplistic terms. Whatever the conflict is, whatever the situation is, I try to simplify it. And it sometimes makes me seem simplistic, and sometimes, perhaps, I am simplistic because of that. Hers is to get into the details, the tiniest little problems of finance, of technology, of everything. So those two types of intelligence worked well together. I have a lot of respect for her organizational abilities. But I'm not going to work with her again in the near future, maybe in the long term future, but not right now.

Q: *What qualities do you think make a good director?*

A: The only consistent quality is high, high energy. I think you need a lot of energy. I think you need to be someone with extraordinary inhuman amounts of energy. It's really the only consistent quality of any achiever in any field.

Q: *Do you have any thoughts for inspiring filmmakers?*

A: You have to be emotionally resilient. To give up is ultimately more work than to keep going. Keep fighting, keep plodding, keep at it, way beyond what's considered human, or natural, or possible. Learn a kind of schizophrenia, where you can be callous to all of the setbacks and still emotionally open so that you can make beautiful films. Separate the industry from the films themselves. That's really important. Realize that it's a privilege to make a movie. Don't think it's your due. Don't think you deserve it. It's a privilege to take that kind of money and tell a story, so treat it with respect. Script, script, script. Get the script right. Ultimately it doesn't matter what kind of reviews you get, people want their money back. It's rude to take money from someone, to borrow it and not give it back. So if you're doing a story that's not going to make a lot of money, keep your budget down. I really think that's part of the elegance of the entire package, that kind of financial responsibility. Be sure to admit what you don't know, especially technically. If you don't feel strong that way, ask and ask and ask. It's not an embarrassment not to know. It's an embarrassment to pretend you know and then get it wrong, a huge embarrassment. Read technical magazines. I read *American Cinematographer* ads just to keep an awareness of the pieces of the machinery. Try to find a logic in that, a beauty in the way the machinery of film-making fits together. To be really, really good, the project has to be more important than life. That doesn't necessarily make you a great person.

The point is to make films that are "great persons," films that have so much personality, such a life, so much truth, and a gen-uine nature. That has to be your highest goal of all. Try always to remember that the kernel of the story, the initial thing that caught you, that affected you, that gave you emotion, that's the thing that you have to fight tooth and nail to hang on to all the way through. Only do what you're proud of. So many people get sucked into doing stuff that they're not proud of and that's who they become. I'm not saying you can't have made a mistake in your direction, or out of desperation had to do certain things, but if at all possible try to resist doing things that you're not really, really proud to have your name on, or that reflect your soul and your personality. There's so many bitter people working. Do any-thing you can do to avoid bitterness, because with bitterness you're dead, everything's dead.

FIFTEEN

Susan Seidelman

Filmography

And You Act Like One Too (1979), Short NYU

Deficit (1980), Short NYU

Yours Truly, Andrea G. Stern (1980), Short NYU

Smithereens (1982), New Line Cinema

Desperately Seeking Susan (1985), Orion

Making Mr. Right (1987), Orion

Cookie (1988), Lorimar Film Entertainment

She-Devil (1989), Orion

Susan Seidelman was born in Philadelphia and grew up in the middle-class suburb of Huntington Valley. Interested in the arts, Seidelman went to the Drexel Institute of Technology to study design. It was there that she took a communications class and became hooked on movies after seeing such films as *Wild Strawberries, The 400 Blows,* and *Breathless.* After graduating from design, she enrolled in the film course at New York University, making three award-winning shorts.

The success of the student films paved the way to her feature film directorial debut, *Smithereens.* This off-beat film about a middle-class dropout who would stop at nothing to achieve fame and a rock star on the decline was made for a meager $80,000 and became the first American independent film to be shown as part of the official competition at the Cannes Film Festival. Although she became the sweetheart of the American independent film scene, it was two years before she directed her next feature, *Desperately Seeking Susan.* It was Barbara Boyle, an executive at Orion Pictures, who fought hard to give Seidelman the break to direct her first studio picture. *Susan* is a film about a bored housewife, played by Rosanna Arquette, who, after a bump on the head, gets amnesia and ends up switching identities with a streetwise punk rocker played by Madonna. Known for her quirky casting, Seidelman had the foresight to cast Madonna in the film just before she rose to the status of international star. The film was a major box office success, and artistically heralded as well.

Her next film, *Making Mr. Right,* is a romantic comedy about a sophisticated professional woman named Frankie, played by Ann Magnuson, who falls in love with an android named Ulysses, played by John Malkovich. Then came *Cookie,* starring Emily Lloyd as an extremely funny and appealing Mafia princess, and *She-Devil,* a tale about a downtrodden housewife (Rosanne Barr) who rises from the ashes of domestic apathy to torment the author (Meryl Streep) who stole her husband.

Although her latest films have not attracted the degree of attention or success at the box office as her first three, Seidelman has firmly established herself as a commentator on modern culture with comic flare.

Q: *How did you get into filmmaking?*

A: When I was a kid I wasn't very interested in films at all. In fact, I didn't see too many films outside of the ones that showed at the shopping mall cinema. I originally thought I wanted to be a designer, specifically a fashion designer. I went to school for that, then somewhere around the age of nineteen or twenty, I got sick of cutting patterns and sewing. So, I took a film course, because it would give me three credits, and I'd get to watch some movies. I got hooked! At that time I hadn't made a film and I didn't know if I could make one, but I knew that I liked to watch them. On a whim I applied to a number of film schools, and got rejected from most, but was accepted to NYU. I also wanted to live in New York, so school was a good excuse to do that. I went to NYU film school, started making short films, and as soon as I started making films I knew that this was something I wanted to do for the rest of my life.

Q: *How do you choose your material?*

A: I like different kinds of things, but I think I'm obsessed with modern life. I am fascinated by pop culture, and the media and the way the media affects how we look at the world around us. Most of the films that I've made, and will continue to make, will in some way be about how we live now in modern times.

Q: *Would you say that you make personal films, or that you look for characters who portray a personal side of you?*

A: I do think that my films are personal to some extent and that the characters, especially the leading ladies in my films, all have elements of me in them. There's a part of me, for example, in *Desperately Seeking Susan*. Like the housewife in the film, my background is very suburban. In fact, I'm a suburban girl. I grew up in one of those nice suburban developments that popped up all over America in the early 1960s, where there's a split level house, a ranch house, and a colonial house. We lived in the colonial house. We lived right around the corner from the shopping mall. And like the character in the film, there was a part of me that knew very early on that I wanted to get out of suburbia. That's why, in a movie like *Desperately Seeking Susan*, one of the reasons the script appealed to me right from the beginning was because it was really about two different sides of me — the suburban person who was kind of bored and dissatisfied with her life, and then also another part of me that maybe was a little more adventurous and could relate to the Madonna character.

Q: *Your first feature film,* Smithereens, *was a project that you generated. How did that happen?*

A: *Smithereens* was made in 1979. I had graduated from film school in 1977. I had been making short films and I knew that I wanted to make a feature, narrative film. But I'm also somewhat realistic in the sense that I knew that if I went to Hollywood and started knocking on doors, no one would hire me to do that. I also had no desire to live in Los Angeles. So I stayed friendly with the same group of people that I'd worked on the short films with, and we decided that if we pooled our resources and didn't get paid, that with a limited amount of money we'd be able to make a low budget feature film. Originally our hope was that the film would be a nice portfolio piece, something to show around in the hopes of getting other work. We never really anticipated getting a commercial release. But when the film was finished it ended up going to the Cannes Film Festival. We were lucky in that it was the first low-budget American film ever to be invited into the official competition section of the festival. It got a lot of attention and a commercial release. The ball kind of started rolling from there.

Q: *After* Smithereens, *what type of scripts did you start looking for?*

A: I'm not a director for hire, so the chances of me finding a script that is exactly what I want to direct are pretty slim. And because I don't write my own material, I have to read a lot of stuff and think about the kinds of films I would be interested in making before I plunge into something. The actual making of the film is an interesting process, but the story better be about something that I really feel strongly about because its too much hard work. There are some directors that just like the activity of making a film. I don't. I find parts of it interesting and parts of it exhausting. It's really the subject matter that appeals to me, or the tone of the movie that appeals to me. So it better be about something that I like. Since I don't write my own material, it takes me a while to find a script that even has a kernel of an idea that would be something that I'd want to spend the next two years of my life working on.

Q: *Why did you choose to do* Desperately Seeking Susan?

A: When I got the script for *Desperately Seeking Susan*, the central idea was something that really appealed to me right from the start. The idea of these two different characters, the suburban housewife and the city/bad girl, was something that had been an issue with me all my life. I'd been brought up to think in terms of "good girls" and "bad girls", and I never knew exactly where I fit within that division. So right from the beginning, the theme appealed to me. The script was originally written in about 1974. It was about a subculture that no longer existed in New York in 1982, which was the year I got the script.

One of the characters was supposed to be a cutting edge kind of character, and culture changes so fast, that what was considered cutting edge in 1974 was no longer cutting edge in 1982. So revisions had to be made. I think the main character of Susan in the original script was much more of a hippie, a bit of a flower child. That was interesting when the script was written, but it would have seemed a little anachronistic by the time the film had come out.

Q: *Did* Desperately Seeking Susan *make you an overnight success?*

A: No. I don't think I'm an overnight success. I've been doing this for about ten years really. It's weird because you'll often hear somebody say that an actress or an actor is an overnight success. That often discounts the fact that they might have been knocking on doors for six years before they became an overnight success. Ever since I started film school, I've been making films. I started in about 1974, then *Smithereens* was released in 1982, and

Desperately Seeking Susan was finished in 1984. So really, that's about a ten year period since I first started making short films, and ten years isn't overnight.

Q: *Was it a difficult transition to make? From directing a low-budget film like* Smithereens *to a big budget picture like* Desperately Seeking Susan?

A: I don't think the transition from *Smithereens* to *Desperately Seeking Susan* was actually as bad as I thought it was going to be. I thought I'd be scared to death. I think it was smooth mainly because I surrounded myself with people whom I was really comfortable with. For example, the director of photography that I worked with, Ed Lockman, was someone who had done a lot of independent low budget films. He wasn't a Hollywood cameraman who was seventy years old and had done fifty studio movies. He was definitely somebody whose background was similar to my own. And the producers also were first-timers, so they weren't these middle-aged guys chomping on fat cigars. Almost straight across the board, with a lot of people that worked on the movie, it was their first time out. So we were all learning together. I was also a little nervous because it was my first time working with a large crew, and I had this preconceived notion about what they were going to be like. I was scared to death that they would see me walk on the set, and here I am, I was about thirty-one years old at the time, and I'm about five feet tall and don't look all that intimidating, and I was afraid that they'd look at me and laugh. But they were a wonderful crew. After the first day they realized that I knew what I was talking about, and a sense of mutual respect evolved.

Q: *Are there any difficulties that you face in the industry that are specific to being a woman?*

A: It was interesting on *Desperately Seeking Susan*, because to some extent the men actually turned out to be in the minority in that production. The executive in charge of the production was a woman named Barbara Boyle at Orion Pictures, the director was a woman, there were two women producers, and the leads were both women. So in a way being a woman on that movie was never an issue because there were so many of us. It's hard to say whether that made it easier or harder. I would deal with the producers not as women but as my producers, and they would deal with me not as a woman but as the director. Whatever arguments we had about the work or whatever, if I wanted to change a location and they liked the present one better, those arguments weren't really gender related.

Q: *Has being a woman had a great impact on your career?*

A: I don't think being a woman director has had a huge impact one way or another, except in terms of the actual work. I think that my films are very much from a female perspective. But in terms of my career progression, because I started out as an independent and generated the first project myself, being a woman wasn't really an issue. Then in *Desperately Seeking Susan* I was in a fortunate situation in that being a woman really was an advantage, because there were so many other woman involved in the project.

Then, because *Susan* was successful, being a woman wasn't an issue anymore. I had proven myself in the marketplace. When you look at the statistics of how many women are actually directing feature films, it's pretty horrendous. Let's face it, Hollywood is still run by men. Hollywood is a business and if monkeys were directing movies that were commercially successful, Hollywood would have monkeys directing movies.

Q: *Has there ever been anyone instrumental in your career?*

A: There have been different people along the way who have been instrumental, I would definitely have to say most instrumental in the leap between *Smithereens* and *Desperately Seeking Susan*. There have been several women that have directed independent features, but because Hollywood is so conservative it's harder to make the leap from independent to studio features. The fact that there was a woman production executive at Orion at that time, in 1983 or 1984, right before *Desperately Seeking Susan*, she was the one who gave me the go-ahead, that was probably pretty instrumental. Her name was Barbara Boyle, and her goal was to try to get women to direct more movies.

Susan Seidelman directing a scene
from *Making Mr. Right*

Q: *What qualities do you look for when choosing actors?*

A: I like kind of off-beat casting, or non-traditional casting, seeing somebody in a role that you wouldn't imagine in that particular role. For example, in *Making Mr. Right*, the lead actor is John Malkovich, an actor who's usually thought of as a dramatic actor, and this is a comedy. For me it was real exciting to work with a dramatic actor in a comedic part. And the leading lady is Ann Magnuson, who has never really done the lead in a studio feature film before. She's well known as a performance artist. She was cast not so much because of her acting ability, but because there was something interesting about her as a person that I wanted to try to get on celluloid. That's the same reason that Madonna was cast in *Desperately Seeking Susan*. I believe that if somebody's interesting, hopefully you can get some of what makes them unique onto the film, and if you can then it's more exciting than using a traditional actor or actress.

Q: *How did you come to cast Madonna in the role of Susan?*

A: Madonna was relatively unknown when I first saw her for

Desperately Seeking Susan. What first impressed me was that she had an aura about her, and a kind of confidence that I thought would be really interesting for the character of Susan to have.

There was something about her that I could see this housewife played by Rosanna Arquette finding really appealing, because it was so different than the quality that Rosanna seemed to have. I remember when I told Orion about Madonna, they didn't know who she was, and they encouraged me to try other actresses who were more famous, because they wanted to get a name — what they called a name — in that part. When we first started filming, Madonna was much less well known than Rosanna Arquette was. Then in the course of filming, over about a nine week period, it was kind of phenomenal how she went from being relatively unknown to being on the cover of *Rolling Stone* magazine. Then by the time we finished the film and it was about to be released, she was on the cover of *Time* or *Newsweek*.

Q: *Did Madonna's rising popularity create problems for you on the set?*

A: It was probably a little more difficult for me working with Rosanna at that time. I wasn't as experienced working with actors or actresses, so I'm sure some of that was my problem. Working with actors is something that you learn by doing it and I really hadn't done much then. In *Smithereens* most of the cast were non-professional or beginning actors. So the fact that Rosanna had been in several more films than I had made, meant that I still had a lot to learn.

Also the fact that Rosanna was the star and Madonna the co-star, I think, made Rosanna a little bit more sensitive to the work. It made everyone a little more on edge. So those things, coupled with the fact that it was the first time that I was making a studio feature, probably made some of the working situations a little more tense.

Q: *Have you improved as a director over the years?*

A: Interesting question. I think that on a technical level I've gotten a little more confident over the years. In the beginning, I didn't think that I had to understand things about lighting or about camera movement, things like that. Now I'm not intimidated by the equipment as much. Maybe some of that came from some weird phobia that I had growing up about how girls are supposed to think equipment is intimidating or technology is scary. But once you get over that, you realize that those are the tools of your trade. If you're going to be intimidated by the equipment, maybe you should think about doing something else. So on that level I feel a lot more comfortable. I also feel a lot more comfortable working with actors. I used to think that there was a secret language, and I thought, "Maybe I have to go the Actors' Studio and learn method acting technique in order to be able to deal with the actors on the set." Now it's not quite as mysterious as I once thought it was.

Often, by being specific about what I think the scene needs or what I think the character needs, I get the feeling or the point across. Being direct and specific often helps.

Q: *What qualities make a good director?*

A: One of the things that makes a good director is having an overview of the total project. There's sometimes a temptation to get lost in one particular element, a small detail. I do think that details are important, but sometimes you can lose track of the overall picture which can be harmful. For me, it's the ability to stand back and watch everything that's going on, not just one particular performance, but all the different elements of the different characters relating to each other within a particular frame. Having an overview of the whole story so that you don't place too little or too much importance in any given thing is good. If you're going to place a lot of importance on any given thing, you better have a good reason for doing that.

Q: *Are there any directors who have influenced you, or whose work you particularly like?*

A: There are a lot of directors that I like, and most of them are directors that have a strong personal point of view in their work. I like Martin Scorsese's work a lot because his work has a certain texture to it. Other directors I like are Fellini, especially his early films like *Nights of Cabiria* and *La Strada.* I like comedies. I like the comedies of Billy Wilder and Preston Sturges. I love B-movies, I'm a real B-movie addict. I love movies like *The Thing with Two Heads.* A great movie I think was a Ray Milan and Rosey Greer picture, where Rosey Greer's head is stuck on Ray Milan's body and Ray Milan is a bigot. All the old Roger Corman movies or Samuel Arkoff movies because those are the movies I grew up watching at the local drive-in. For me, I like a mix of highbrow stuff and real lowbrow stuff. It's the movies in the middle that I'm not as interested in, because for me those are the movies that are best left to TV.

Q: *What would you say has been the hardest task that you've faced professionally?*

A: I think the hardest time professionally in my life was when I made *Smithereens.* There were a lot of negative things that happened right at the beginning of making that movie. When I started *Smithereens*, I knew that I wanted to do a feature film, but I had no money. I never knew how to budget properly for a feature, so originally I raised about $25,000 or $30,000 and thought that I could make an entire feature for that amount. We planned on shooting for about five weeks, and by the end of the second week we'd used up about $20,000.

I had no idea where we were going to get the rest of the money to finish the shoot. Then about two days after that we were rehearsing and the leading actress, Susan Berman, fell off a fire escape during a rehearsal and broke her leg. So, here I was with no money, with the leading lady in a cast, and with a crew I wasn't paying. I thought, "There's no way that I'm going to be able to hold them all together until she gets out of the cast three or four months from now." But when there's something that I really need to do, there's a part of me that gets real determined because I feel like everything is against me. I get this "I'm gonna show you" kind of attitude. And in a way it pushes me to be a little bit more resourceful, because I feel like the world is against me at that moment. One of the things that happened at that time was the opportunity to turn a very negative experience into a very positive experience. I had a chance to re-write the script for the specific actors I was now using, and also to raise more money. Up until that point I had only directed short films, and I think that when you do a short film and you're working very intensely for two weeks or so, you pace yourself differently than you do if you're working for five or six weeks. For example, during short films we would eat pizza everyday and take-out Chinese food for two weeks. If you try doing that over a five week period, you get really unhealthy, really exhausted. I just assumed that for five weeks we would eat pizza, and everyone would be happy. But by the tenth day of pizza there was mutiny. So having some time off to really think about the differences between a feature and a short film turned out positive.

I think ultimately it made *Smithereens* much more successful than it would have otherwise been had she not broken her leg.

Q: *What would you say has been your biggest triumph?*

A: One of the most up moments in my life has to be the Cannes Film Festival in 1982. I went there with *Smithereens*, and had no idea what the Cannes Film Festival was. I had heard of it. I knew it was a festival that was important, but I really didn't realize the full importance of it. I thought that you fly to France, you show your movie, people applaud or they boo, and then you go home. I didn't really realize that a festival like that could launch your career in a much more long-term way. So I was kind of naive when I went to Cannes, but I learned a lot by being there. For example, in terms of international distribution — I knew nothing about that until I got there. For me, the benefit of these kinds of festivals is enormous, especially as an independent filmmaker. What they do really is give you the opportunity to show your work to a world cinema market. People from all over the world who love movies get to see your work and that experience is invaluable.

Q: *What is the greatest difficulty you have had to overcome as a director?*

A: One of the hardest things was learning how to talk to actors, because it was something I just wasn't used to. In particular, I think that it was a little difficult for me working with Rosanna at times because of the tension around Madonna. There were a couple of times when I think perhaps if I were a man, or maybe if I were a father figure, or maybe even if I were more of a mother figure, I could have talked to her in a more comforting way. My approach with people is not maternal at all really. I try to be direct with people. If there's something that I want, I think that the honest and earthy approach usually works. But with some people it doesn't. So at times our relationship got a little tense.

There was one time on the set, the scene where Rosanna goes to the Port Authority Bus Station after she's gotten hit on the head and she's got amnesia. Right before we did that scene, there was a question about how much amnesia Rosanna should play. Should she play it with realistic amnesia, or just a little bit disoriented, but not medically correct. We might have disagreed about the level to play that. There was also some tension in the air around the whole shooting process at that time. And we had one of these "I hate you," "I hate you," "I hate you," "I hate the movie," sort of dialogues. Suddenly I just burst out crying. And she had burst out crying too. The producer came over and was trying to mediate between Rosanna and myself, and the next thing I know the producer started crying.

It was embarrassing because here was the lead actress, the director, and the producer all standing around crying, with maybe a hundred extras in the background watching us. But what was nice was that after we all pulled ourselves together, there was something kind of catharsis that happened.

Q: *What attracted you to* Making Mr. Right?

A: The basic idea of it. It was set in Miami. It had a story that I thought I could tell in a certain way, with a certain tone that would be a little different than anything I'd done before. *Smithereens* and *Desperately Seeking Susan* were set in New York and I didn't want to repeat myself. I think one of the dangers that all directors have to fight against is repeating things because they're effective. After a while you start getting lazy. I didn't want that to happen. So I intentionally wanted to make a movie some place else.

I also liked the idea in *Making Mr. Right*, and the period is kind of obscure. It's sort of the present, but it's sort of the future, the future from the point of 1962 or 1963. The idea of doing something that had an element of science fiction to it, but wasn't going to look like a slick high-tech movie, appealed to me. Another thing that appealed to me was a technical challenge that the movie proposed. I intentionally wanted to work with special effects, but I didn't want to use them in a *Star Wars* kind of slick way. The story appealed to me. It's a movie about a woman who ends up falling in love with a robot.

I have no interest in making a robot movie, or an android movie, but I like the metaphor of an android as a blank slate of a man. The way the Chauncy Gardener character was in *Being There*. Somebody who's very innocent and reflects the world around them. So the idea of this blank innocent person appealed to me.

Q: *Do you consider your filmmaking political?*

A: I think my films are more sociological in a way than they are political, really. I'm interested in the way the culture changes. If I wasn't a filmmaker I'd probably want to be either a painter or a sociologist. Because I am really fascinated by the way people act, the way they talk, the way they dress, and the kinds of things they do in their spare time. I'm also very, very interested in modern life and how we think now.

SIXTEEN

Joan
Micklin Silver

Filmography

Hester Street (1975), Midwest Films

Bernice Bobs Her Hair (1976), Short

Between the Lines (1977), Midwest Films

Head Over Heels a.k.a *Chilly Scenes Of Winter* (1979), United Artists

Finnegan Begin Again (1985), Tron-EMI/HBO TV

Crossing Delancey (1988), Warner Brothers

Loverboy (1989), Tri-Star Pictures

Prison Stories: Women on the Inside (1991), Segment, HBO TV

Joan Micklin Silver began her film career in the late 1960s by writing educational and children's film scripts for Encyclopedia Britannica and the Learning Corporation of America. She also directed three shorts for the LCA: *The Case of the Elevator Duck, The Fur Coat,* and *The Immigrant Experience.* In 1972, with the help of *Dirty Dancing* producer Linda Gottlieb, Silver sold a screenplay entitled *Limbo* to Universal Pictures. Although successful as a writer, she wanted to direct. Her attempts were met with great opposition during the very audaciously sexist period of the 1970s. In spite of the rejections, Silver was determined to get her shot. She formed Midwest films with her husband Ray Silver, and in 1975 he raised the financing for Joan to make her feature film directorial debut with the small, independent film *Hester Street.* The film was made for under $400,000. Although it was initially rejected by many distributors, the film became a critical success, earning over five million dollars and an Oscar nomination for its star Carol Kane.

Joan Silver has since been successful in the difficult transition from independent filmmaker to major studio director, although it wasn't easy at first. After directing *Between the Lines,* another feature for her own company, she was hired by United Artists to direct *Chilly Scenes of Winter.* This partnership eventually ensued in a battle between Silver and the studio. Not only did the studio change the title of the picture to *Head Over Heels,* they even changed the ending, against Joan's wishes. After that experience Silver did some directing in theater and television. In 1988 she returned to the big screen with the very successful *Crossing Delancey,* which starred Amy Irving. Joan isn't the only filmmaker in the family. Her husband Ray is a producer/director. One of the films he directed, *On The Yard,* was produced by their oldest daughter Dina, and another daughter, Marisa, is a successful director of features such as *Permanent Record* and *He Said/She Said* for Paramount Pictures.

$\mathbf{Q}$: *How did you become a filmmaker?*

A: My original game plan was to write movies that would all be brought to the screen by the great directors, and I would learn how to direct as I went along. Then, at the perfect, proper time, I would step out myself and I would direct. Of course that fantasy didn't come true. The first film I sold to Hollywood was *Limbo* which was meant to be a gritty story of the wives of POWs and MIAs in Vietnam, sort of an early anti-Vietnam piece based on research conducted with real wives of POWs and MIAs. It was sold to Universal and made into a film by Mark Robson. He had a different vision of the film than me. He was entitled to have his own vision of the film. I realized that it didn't make sense to keep writing scripts and let other people's visions of my films get onto the screen. I wanted to put my own vision up there.

Q: *Were you at all involved in the production of* Limbo?

A: Mark had been extremely generous, and invited me to visit the set. I spent nine days there. By that time I had been replaced by another screenwriter. But I still had this constant inclination as I watched the scenes to say, "No, no, no." It wasn't that he wasn't doing what he should have been doing, which was to use his own choices, and his own rhythms, and his own camera placements, and all the rest, it's just that I saw the whole story so differently.

So I went out and tried to seek a job directing. But in those years, and this is the early '70s — 71, 72, 73 — in that time, the barriers against women directors were very much present. And although I could get work as a screenwriter, I had absolutely no chance of getting work as a director. I mean in one case I tried to get a job directing on television. I had written the script, the producer loved the script, absolutely wanted to do it, but he told me that in good conscience he couldn't hire me because the longest film I had done was thirty-one minutes and an hour TV show was forty-six minutes. It was things like that, such phony kinds of excuses that made me feel like walking around the avenue screaming and tearing my hair out.

Q: *How did you get started?*

A: My husband Ray, a real estate developer, was watching my struggle. It made him angry and he thought it was unfair. He told me that he thought everybody should at least have a chance to try for the brass ring. I remember exactly those words. He said if I could write a screenplay that would be very low budget, he would try to raise the money and produce it for me so I could direct it. That was how *Hester Street* happened. That was the first feature film I did.

Q: *Why did you choose* Hester Street *as your first film?*

A: Just before I made *Hester Street*, I was quite discouraged at that point about the possibilities of ever making a feature film. I thought just in case this is the only one I ever get to make, I'd like to make one that had a personal meaning to my family. *Hester Street* is about Russian-Jewish immigrants and my family, although not from the lower east-side, had been Russian-Jewish immigrants. I'd grown up on stories around the dinner table of immigrant lives and adventures. I always thought they were incredibly dramatic and an important part of American history that seemed not to be addressed in film very much.

Q: *How did you develop* Hester Street?

A: I love to do research. One of the great pleasures I had was reading a lot of immigrant literature, not only of Jewish immigrants, but Polish immigrants, Russian immigrants, and Irish immigrants. A tremendous wealth of stories. I even went to the Yiddish Institute in New York. There's a series of unpublished oral reports which immigrants have simply given to the institute which it has collected and translated. What I didn't want to do was somehow cheat the people who were alive who had had the experience. And I didn't want them to go to the movie and say, "Oh, it was nothing like that." I myself have had experiences and seen movies that seemed to be so remote from the reality that I know. It's anger provoking. One of the things that pleased me the most about *Hester Street* was that a number of old immigrant people told me they thought that I'd gotten it right, or at least part of it right, the part of it I was trying to do.

Q: *How was* Hester Street *received?*

A: When we finished *Hester Street* we took it around to various distributors. Naturally we had alleged to our investors, most of whom were people who had invested in Ray's real estate ventures, that we would of course be able to get the film released. But when the majors saw it they felt it was a black and white film with Yiddish and subtitles and nobody in it, and the usual things like that, which majors think about. And the minor distributors at that time seemed to feel that the best thing they could do was to put it out in 16mm and hit the synagogue circuit, maybe colleges. These things bothered us a lot, because by that time the film had gone to Cannes and had done extremely well. We sold the rights ourselves in four countries and that gave us enough money to open in New York. So at that point we became distributors and that's how Midwest Films got into the distribution business. Fortunately *Hester Street* did very well at the box office.

I remember the opening date of the film particularly because we had been told by those "in the know" that what you should hope for on the opening day of your film is neither bad weather, which will keep people at home, nor very good weather, which will take them to the park. What you want is something kind of gray. So we got up that day and it was pouring. It was a Sunday. Ray said, "Well I'm going to watch the football game, I'm not going to put myself through this. I'm not going to go down there and see how nobody's going to come to the theater." But in fact, somebody who we knew called us and said, "You should come down." We went down there and it was just lines of umbrellas going around the block. Carol Kane was the star and her mother came down and took pictures of the lines around the block so we'd have it recorded for all time. The film went on to do really well. Carol got an Academy Award nomination, which was fantastically helpful to the film, and allowed it to move from a small art film circuit to a very wide break.

Q: *How much did it cost to make* Hester Street *and has it earned a profit?*

A: It cost $320,000. Honestly I don't know at this point how

Joan Micklin Silver directing
Crossing Delancey, with Amy Irving

much it's made. I mean, it's been a number of years and I haven't kept up with it, but it's an example of an extraordinarily successful independent film.

Q: *Did you have children when you made the film?*

A: Yes. During those days my children were young, and being a mother, I was always dragging them with me to auditions or whatever else I was doing. And they ended up learning a lot about filmmaking. In fact, I've often felt that's the difference between male and female filmmakers. When people say is there a difference between men filmmakers and women filmmakers, I say, "Yes, because women's children will always be on the set because they don't have anywhere else to take them." During the time the kids were on the set they had a very good time. They were very well-treated by crews and cast and they made a lot of friends. You could see that they were all getting quite interested in the process, particularly the middle daughter. There are three girls. The three are Dina, Marisa, and Claudia, and the middle girl, Marisa, was totally hooked on the whole thing. She was the one who wanted to read every draft of every screenplay and she was the one who'd say, "Oh please, please can I leave school and come along for just this one audition? I'll go right back to school." You could see at an early age she was quite into the process. The youngest girl, Claudia, always wanted to be an actress. The oldest one, Dina, didn't necessarily seem to be one thing or another, although I said when she was about thirteen that I thought some day Dina would run something. I didn't know if it would be a school or a battleship, but she always had a lot of organizational skills. Anyway, by the time Marisa got to high school, she began directing and made a documentary. She went on to Harvard and made a film there.

Then she had a chance to make a documentary and left Harvard to do it. She then decided that she wanted to make a feature film based on an experience that she had as a young girl. She wrote the script and got into Sundance, which is an institute that helps young filmmakers and gives them a chance to learn more about the skills that they have. She phoned Dina who was living out in Oakland, California at the time and asked Dina if she would produce the film and come to Sundance with her. Dina said, "Well let me read the script." Dina did and agreed to do it. They ended up actually producing, directing, and writing *Old Enough,* which was a wonderful film. It was released by Orion Classics, and was Marisa's debut film.

Q: *Has the whole family continued in filmmaking?*

A: Marisa now lives in California, where she is directing feature films for the major studios. Ray started out producing and the first two films he produced of mine were *Hester Street* and *Between the Lines.* But unfortunately, it took him about fifteen minutes to find out that my job was better than his job. I made the mistake of letting him do some second unit shots on *Hester Street,* and he loved it. It was sort of like a taste of blood; the minute you see what it's like you want to do it yourself. And when we finished *Between the Lines* he told me that he would like to direct the next one. So he found a script, actually a book, called *On the Yards,* a prison story, by Malcolm Bailey, who has been in prison himself. He and Malcolm worked on the script and together made the film. He's since gone on to make a film called *A Walk on the Moon* which Dina produced. Dina's a very good producer.

Q: *Did you give your daughters any advice?*

A: In a way I was flattered that they enjoyed doing what I was doing, and that they were interested in the field. I'd rather see my children seek out professions which are under-populated, in which there is too much work for too few people, thereby assuring them work, economic security and so on. But at the same time I don't think any of them entered the film business with a particularly overly-rosy view of it. At numerous discussions around the dinner table they've met a lot of actors, directors, designers and so on that have laid out the realities of the business. I think that all of them have a realistic picture of what it's like.

Q: *What are the qualities of a good director?*

A: A strong sensibility and something to say. I know that one of the complaints I hear from some of my friends who teach at film school is that they often find kids who are very skilled technically, they all got Super-8 cameras when they were four, the next one when they were six, and they've all got a lot of technical know-how, but they don't know anything about life and literature and all the rest.

When it was time for Marisa to go to college, she asked me if I thought she should go to film school or to college? And I said, "Well, what do you think?" And she said, "I think I should go to college." And I said, "Boy, so do I because there's a lot to life besides film stock and so on. There's a lot of great literature. There's history. There's so many things to learn, to know about." I think that the best filmmakers are the people who are immersed in life and not just technique.

Q: *How have you changed as a director?*

A: I guess the interesting thing about directing is that although you may get a little better at it, in the sense that certain problems you've coped with before you can cope with again, still every time you do it's like jumping off a cliff. Every time it's the unknown. And I think although it's the thing you complain about as a director, it's probably the thing that is so much fun. I don't think of myself as a person who likes to jump off cliffs. Yet I guess I do because the whole mystery of how it comes together, how this one plays with that one, how a scene which maybe didn't quite read right becomes adjusted on the set and somehow begins to play beautifully or whatever. That's the magic of it and the part that's so exciting.

Q: *What about working with the studios?*

A: The thing about the studios right now in America is that the studios tend to develop a great, great, great many projects for every project that they do. This leads to all the stories that you read about people who have written very good screenplays, gotten paid for every one, never had one made, but still had the house in Santa Monica or wherever it is. I'm interested in making movies, and that's one aspect of studio work that I don't like as much. But I continue to be offered things by the studios and to entertain projects, and I have no problems at all. I'll be glad to make movies with anybody who gives me the money to make them.

Q: *Do you like working with actors?*

A: One of the directors I've always admired is Elia Kazan, particularly for his work with actors. Some of the great film performances that I have seen have been under his direction. I had spent a lot of time before I had a chance to direct, certainly in the early years of directing, reading all these terrific film books which gave you interviews with directors in which they talked about their experiences. Kazan said that on a film the director should have a "mono-mono" very early during principal photography with the main actor, and the director must win it. So I tucked this away but it never seemed to be happening to me.

Then I got to the set of *Chilly Scenes of Winter*, which is a story about a young man's obsession for a married woman and the lengths that it drives him to. It's a comedy. We were doing a scene, a dinner table scene. John Heard was the main character. He played Charles, the man with the obsession. There were others at the dinner table as well. We did a large complicated master and then we started to do the coverage on it. I hadn't done a lot of masters and coverage in that particular film, but in the case of this scene I did. We got to doing singles and I said, "Cut! John what you're doing here doesn't match what you've done in the master." He said, "So What?" And I thought, "Oh, the mono-mono, it's here, it's here." So I said "Well, so what it is, is that I like it better the other way." He said, "Oh, okay." That was the entire mono-mono.

Q: *Do you find it hard being a woman in a predominantly male industry?*

A: It's hard for me to say. I haven't worked in any business that's predominantly female, so I don't know what that would be like. I think people rather misunderstand what it is that a director does. A director doesn't stand there and say to the third grip, "Now you move this." Basically you're communicating with your director of photography, your production designer, and the other heads of departments. And these people are conveying their thoughts to their people, their particular crews.

So what the groups do, what the electricians do and so on, is pretty much under the guidance of the department heads. The crews that I've worked with are people who want to do good work, and they want to make good films. So I don't think they care who's at the helm, as long as somebody knows what they're doing and has some ideas to convey on film. That's been my experience.

SEVENTEEN

Penelope
Spheeris

Filmography

Real Life (1978), Producer

The Decline of Western Civilization (1979), Documentary

Suburbia (1982), New World Pictures

The Boys Next Door (1985), New World Pictures

Hollywood Vice Squad (1986), Cinema Group

Dudes (1987), New Century/Vista Film Co.

The Decline of Western Civilization: The Metal Years (1989), Documentary

Prison Stories: Women on the Inside (1991), Segment, HBO TV

Wayne's World (1992), Paramount Pictures

The Beverly Hillbillies (1993), Twentieth Century-Fox

Penelope Spheeris spent the first half dozen years of her life on the road, traveling with a circus troupe where her father was a strongman and her mother a ticket vendor. Her father was murdered when she was seven, and subsequently her mother moved the family to the suburbs of Orange County, California, where Spheeris grew up. Her interest in film began after she switched from Behavioral Psychology to Theater Arts while attending UCLA in the early 1970s. When Spheeris graduated in 1973, the outlook for women directors in Hollywood was bleak. She found work as an editor with an educational film company. A year later she formed Rock 'n' Reel, her own independent company, and one of the first to make music videos. She directed for bands such as Fleetwood Mac, Ry Cooder, The Funkadelics, and many others before becoming dissatisfied with "making commercials."

Her next job was for Lorne Michael's *Saturday Night Live* producing the classic series of short films directed by Albert Brooks. Brooks later engaged Spheeris as producer of his pseudo-documentary satire, *Real Life*. With her first feature film credit under her belt, she returned to directing. In 1979, she released *The Decline of Western Civilization*, a feature documentary on the L.A. punk scene that included performances by X, Black Flag, and The Germs. Next was *Suburbia*, her tough, unrelenting look at the punk generation, and her first fiction film. It was made on a low budget with Roger Corman producing.

Her subsequent film, *The Boys Next Door*, featured Charlie Sheen and Maxwell Caulfield as a pair of ordinary working class boys who end up on a killing spree. In this film, Spheeris attempts to take a look at the explosive violence lurking below the surface of repressed emotions. She followed this with *Hollywood Vice Squad*, an action picture, then *Dudes*, a punk rock western.

In 1989 she returned to her documentary and music roots with the release of *The Decline of Western Civilization: The Metal Years*. The two documentaries are bookends to a decade that produced a total of seven features — a large turnout for any Hollywood director, especially a woman. Spheeris continues to live in L.A. and has most recently completed two top box office hits, *Wayne's World* and *The Beverly Hillbillies*.

Q: *How did you get involved with* Wayne's World? *Did Mike Meyers approach you?*

A: Mike Meyers didn't approach me, Lorne Michaels did. I know Lorne from way back. I was sent an early draft of the script, and I responded to the subject matter and the basic milieu of the picture because I know a lot about both metal music and kids.

Q: *How long were you involved with the project before it went into production?*

A: Luckily they had to shoot really soon after I was approached, so that meant they had to decide on the director right away. I had to go to five meetings with the studio people because it was a difficult process to convince them that I could do a comedy, but since I had done a season on *Roseanne* they felt that I had the background.

Q: *Do you feel that you were given the kind of creative freedom you wanted, given the fact that the format of the original concept was popularized on* Saturday Night Live?

A: I felt fine about it. There's lots of stuff that I know that they don't know. I mean they spend their lives in Rockefeller Plaza Center, way up high, and I spend my life on the street. I don't know why people always ask me that question — do I feel like I got enough input. Yeah. More than I would ever want. Believe me. I had to do a lot on that show.

Q: *What was it like to collaborate with Mike Meyers?*

A: It had its ups and downs. He was kind of nervous because he'd never done a movie before. And since *Wayne's World* was his little conception in the first place, he had a lot on the line.

Q: *Do you storyboard before directing action?*

A: Yes. Whenever I have to do any action sequences, or special effects or stunts, I do a storyboard and stick right with it. It's a communication. It's a way to communicate to the rest of the crew.

Q: *How did you determine the visual attitude of* Wayne's World? *How did you prepare the visual look?*

A: Because there are times when Mike is talking to the TV camera in his little basement studio, and other times when he's talking to the film camera, we had to map all those things out to determine the style. It's pretty complex actually. I took the script and marked it up. I used one color for when he's talking to the real camera and another color for when he's talking to the video camera in the basement. I just mark it up like that. Then I know that we've got to be here for that coverage, and in this other place for the next thing.

Q: *How did you break into the business?*

A: I started with a film company called *Rock 'n' Reel* and I did films for the music business. It was 1974 and I think it was the first film company that did rock videos. I shot a lot of different bands. I stopped doing it in 1977 and produced a feature film.

Q: *Tell me why you wanted to make films.*

A: The reason I wanted to become a director is because I had produced before and I didn't like what you had to do to be a producer, nailing people to the wall for money. Also I did have something of a creative urge, and directing was a good outlet for it.

Q: *What is* Suburbia, *your first dramatic feature film about?*

A: *Suburbia*'s about a bunch of outcast punk rock kids who clash with suburban normalities. After that I made *The Boys Next Door*, which is about a couple of average next door kids who just happen to be serial killers.

Q: *How would you define your style?*

A: For years now I've been known as the rebel filmmaker. I really didn't know that I was coming from that place. I guess I was a teenage rebel or something, and I never quite grew out of it. I would say the kind of filmmaker that I am is somewhat controversial. I remember when *The Decline* came out, it was a small documentary feature and someone made that point.

Q: *Why are your films so violent?*

A: I have a big fascination with anger, why people get so angry and how they let it out. I tried to incorporate that into *The Boys Next Door, Suburbia,* and even *The Decline.* I don't know, there is a lot of violence and there is some nudity and a little bit of sex, but that's part of life and I don't think you can gloss over it, or forget it.

For example what I tried to do with *The Boys Next Door,* as far as the violence was concerned, was to show violence as it really is, rather than showing it in a sort of glorified form like you always get with *Rambo* or Clint Eastwood movies. I tried to show it the way it really is. When I did research for *The Boys Next Door,* I remember one quote from a guy who said, "I couldn't believe when I killed this girl that it took so long." That's because with the media and with films in general we always see violence happening so easily and quickly. Like violence is okay. So, I decided to show it like it wasn't okay. But because of that, I think it really puts a lot of people off. That film didn't get any kind of a release here. It's very well known in Europe, though. My films are much better accepted there. I feel that people don't understand me as a filmmaker because, they think, "Oh, she never compromises and she always has to have those hard core subjects and it's not mainstream." Well, I'm trying to make mainstream films. I have to compromise every day, and I can't make any film I want. There are very few film directors, and especially women film directors, who can make any film they want. People give me scripts and say, "Well let's do it." And I say, "I love the script, but I can't get it made." And they think I'm lying, that I don't like the script.

Q: *Why do you choose the topics that you do?*

A: People are always asking me why I make films that have to do with outcasts and strange people, and I think it's because I was born in a carnival and from a very early age I was exposed to outcasts and freaks. I feel comfortable around them and I feel like I understand them. Besides, somebody's got to do it. I have compassion for the underdogs, the weirdos. I hate television sitcoms because everyone's so normal. The people in my films, I think, are a bit off-beat, but I'm glad about that.

Penelope Spheeris on the set of
Dudes

Q: *Would you say your films are made from a woman's point of view?*

A: No, my films aren't particularly from a woman's point of view. As a matter of fact, people are always saying, "Wait a minute, this looks like a man directed it. What's going on here?" I don't know what's going on, but I think it's just from a human being's point of view, not a man or a woman's point of view. I'm always being criticized because I don't make films that are real sensitive to women's problems and don't deal with women in a way that some people think I should deal with them. But the way I see it is that it's not a woman or a man, it's a person. What is the integrity, or the ups and downs, or the bad and the good about this person? If I was to make a "woman's film," I would like to do the kind of film that is about a strong, determined forceful woman that kicks ass. What can I tell you? I'm not into sci-fi pictures, but Sigourney Weaver in *Aliens* was the closest feminine lead character that I'd be interested in doing a film on. I don't like all that sappy shit.

Q: *How did you get involved with Corman?*

A: I got involved with Roger Corman when he raised half of the

Calling the Shots

budget for *Suburbia*, and he produced it for me. Roger Corman is great. He gave me a list of do's and don'ts for directors. I still have it. I'm gonna sell it someday. Ha, ha. Anyway he sets you down in the beginning and tells you the rules. It's really an education. I think he does it with all of his first time directors. He sets you down and tells you the rules of directing. It actually was quite helpful. He would say for example, "You should always keep the camera moving. Static cameras are not really very interesting. And you always light one side of the room, shoot that, finish it off, then you light the other side of the room, shoot that, finish it off. You never go back and forth, you're wasting your time with the crew. The crew gets very upset about their time being wasted. You never improvise on camera. It's generally a waste of film. And always, as a director, you have to know where your next shot's going to be and even the shot after that." It was good because after that he didn't bother me too much. He just came to the set the first day and he was very open-minded about the cut.

Corman taught me so much about the basics, the real facts about how to direct a picture. His list was one thing and it was cute and nice and helpful, but what I really mean is he encourages you to rehearse the actors, and probably the most important thing that he taught me was how to do a complete and proper shot list. Without a shot list I don't see how you can make a good film.

Q: *What are the qualities of a good director?*

A: The ability to make a fast decision, I believe, because you have about forty people standing around wondering what's happening and they're all looking to you for that answer. Sometimes I think it's better to make a wrong decision than to make a postponed decision or no decision. That's what I've found. As for me, I'm always prepared. I always come to the set with the shot list that I need and I know exactly what has to be done. I get myself involved with all the different areas. I know how the special effects work and how the stunts work, how long all that will take. I take a lot of input from the various departments, because I like to try to integrate different people's ideas into the film. I don't feel that I always know what's best.

222

Q: *Do you prefer collaboration?*

A: What I do is I try to keep an open mind to suggestions. I think my job is to pick out the best suggestions and use them. Then, of course, later take the credit for them.

Q: *Do you find that women filmmakers are competitive with each other?*

A: If a woman film director has a success, then the rest of us work more. It's only sensible that we all work together. I can't believe people think that women filmmakers should be competitive, or are competitive. I certainly don't feel competitive toward any of the other directors, and it would be really self-defeating if I were. The scene in Hollywood now for women directors is really the best it's ever been. The fact is it's almost trendy to hire a woman film director. Finally, it's not a big scare to have a woman directing your picture. There's some confidence there now from the industry. It's about time. I mean I'm five pictures in here.

Q: *Do you think there's a "Boy's Club" in Hollywood?*

A: Is there a "Boy's Club" in Hollywood? Yes. I would have already peaked in my career and be on a downslide by now like most of my male cohorts in school if I hadn't been a woman. I've had to fight harder. I've had to worker harder. I've had to have a cleaner life. In Hollywood if you're a guy and you have a drug habit or an alcohol habit or you don't treat your family right, well that's just the way it is, but if you're a woman and you step out of line, they're going to axe you.

Q: *Do you find it difficult being a woman in this business?*

A: I remember when I had *Rock 'n' Reel*, being at the Beverly Hills Hotel, meeting some guy from CBS Records, and having him literally try to tear my clothes off and say, "Do you want to do the David Essex video on Wednesday or not?" I mean I've been through really degrading situations that could cause a person to hate.

Q: *How do you deal with that?*

A: I've just kept on fighting. I'll tell you another obstacle that I've encountered as far as being a woman. It's been really hard to get my film, *Dudes*, into a decent release. I do believe that if I was a man with a beard and a baseball hat like you're supposed to be if you're a director, they would probably listen to me. I tell them the kind of theaters it belongs in and the release pattern that it should have, but since I'm a woman they think that I don't know what I'm talking about.

Q: *How about on the set? How do you deal with crews?*

A: I don't have too much trouble on the set because I'm very forceful. I have a pretty good reputation and I do have the respect of the crews. I mean, if I have problems I fire people. That's just the bottom line because I'm out to get my job done, and if anybody wants to fuck around with me, then they're out. We'll give their pay cheque to somebody else. That might sound pretty hard-core, but it's what you have to do.

Q: *Can you describe your films and your point of view in them?*

A: There's no reason to make films just for money. I like to make films that deal with social issues. For example, the problems kids have, like with *The Boys Next Door*. It was an exaggeration of where a lot of kids are at, but I hoped it would give some insight, for parents to see why kids end up on the wrong side of the tracks. With *Suburbia* and *The Decline* I was dealing with these punk rock kids who were the outcasts from society.

I think I'm able to relate to those kind of people because I was raised in a carnival where everybody I knew when I was growing up were freaks and outcasts, so to me those are normal people. I don't understand the everyday straight person. I'm not trying hard to be different, I'm just being what I am. I am different. I know that I am different, that I don't think the way most people think. I've had a very difficult life. I've had some tragedies in my life and that affects you. I didn't have a *Father Knows Best* childhood at all. So, I'm a weirdo, okay.

Q: *Do you deal with violence for the same reasons?*

A: Yes, and I think I deal with violence in films in a very realistic way because I've experienced a lot of violence in my own life. I was raised in a very abusive family. Every week somebody was bloody from a fight, and I lived in neighborhoods where violence was a way of life.

Q: *Don't you feel that violence in the media desensitizes the viewer?*

A: Well, I certainly don't want to perpetuate violence, in any way. It's my theory that if you show violence in its true form, it will be repulsive and people won't want to imitate it or recreate it. One fault with most American movies and television is that they make violence look easy and negligible, but it's not that way.

Q: *Do you get a lot of criticism because you portray violence in your films?*

A: When I did *Dudes*, there were a couple of violent scenes, slightly violent scenes in the film. Now I think that if it was a man who directed that film, there would be no mention of the violence, but because I'm a woman who's dealing with violence, all of a sudden it's compounded. Women are not supposed to deal with violence. We're only supposed to be nice and soft and warm and deal with delicate, motherly, feminine things. I think a lot of people are outraged because I've had violent scenes in my films. That's just because I'm a woman. Why don't I have a right to deal with violence? I got slapped around when I was a kid. Why didn't they slap my brothers around instead of me if women aren't supposed to be involved with violence? I was taught violence.

Q: *Has being a filmmaker cost you in your personal life?*

A: The personal sacrifices that I've had to make and probably will continue to make include not being able to give enough time to my daughter whom I have raised all by myself. She's seventeen now. She's been around a lot of movie sets though, so maybe she has learned something. Also, I can't even begin to get along with any guys. It's like I'm always off working too much and they'll say, "Your career is more important than me."

Q: *So, has the success of* Wayne's World *helped your career?*

A: Well, let's just put it like this, the movie made a lot of money, so I guess that helps. But it doesn't make the scripts that you get any better. I still can't find a project I want to do.

Q: *Since making* Wayne's World *are you still considered the rebel filmmaker?*

A: No. My problem now is that since I had a hit comedy, I can only do comedy. Believe it or not, after being unable to get a comedy off the ground for so long, now that's all I'm offered.

Q: *Haven't they seen* Suburbia *or* The Boys Next Door?

A: They've seen them, they just forget about them because they didn't make money. The only thing that counts to them is the fact that I made money with a comedy, so I can only do comedies now. I've found a couple of thrillers I want to do, but I can't do them because there's no comedy in them.

EIGHTEEN

Joan Tewkesbury

Filmography

Thieves Like Us (1975), Screenplay (co-scripted)

Nashville (1977), Screenplay, Paramount Pictures

Old Boyfriends (1978), AVCO Embassy Pictures Corp.

The Tenth Month (1979), CBS TV

The Acorn People (1981), NBC TV

Cold Sassy Tree (1989), Cable TV

Sudie and Simpson (1990), Cable TV

In 1970 Joan Tewkesbury called Robert Altman and asked him for a job. He invited her to come to Vancouver as a script supervisor on *McCabe and Mrs. Miller.* Tewkesbury never looked back. An only child raised in Los Angeles, she has been associated with show business most of her life. Tewkesbury began dance lessons at the age of three, and by age ten she danced in the film *The Unfinished Dancer* with Margaret O'Brien and Cyd Charisse. Her parents divorced when she was in her early teens and Tewkesbury decided to give up dance to lead a 'normal' life, eventually marrying and having two children. At the age of thirty five she made a major decision, to shed her 'normal' life and pursue her career. She gave up her house in Santa Monica, let the kids go live with their father, from whom she was already separated, and set out to find work.

In 1973, after working as a dancer, choreographer, actress, theater director, and script girl, she co-wrote her first feature script, *Thieves Like Us,* co-scripted with Calder Willingham, which Altman directed. Next came *Nashville,* a solo effort, again intended for Altman's direction. *Nashville* tells the story of twenty-four characters who cross paths in and around the country music industry. Tewkesbury carefully intertwined six highly emotional plots that span a five day period. That film brought her critical attention.

She went on to direct her first feature, *Old Boyfriends,* written by Paul Schrader (*Taxi Driver, Raging Bull*). Although the film did not do well, Tewkesbury knew that she wanted to pursue her directing career. Her next two features were made for television. *The Tenth Month,* starring Carol Burnette, looks at a middle-aged woman who has got to come to terms with herself after discovering that she's pregnant, and *The Acorn People* looks at the lives of a group of handicapped children at summer camp.

Tewkesbury continues to develop feature film projects while directing for television and teaching script writing at UCLA.

$\mathbf{Q}$: *Why did you become a writer?*

A: Out of a desire to direct. I believed that writing would be my entrance. I had been working with Altman on *McCabe and Mrs. Miller*, and realized that to write a screenplay, you didn't have to think of the whole three acts, that screenplays are really made up of small sections of scenes. I wrote my first screenplay based on the fact that I was getting a divorce. I gave it to Altman, and he gave me the opportunity to adapt a book for him, *Thieves Like Us*. From there I wrote *Nashville*, but I've always felt desperate to get to the directing.

Q: *Where did the idea for the structure of* Nashville *come from?*

A: I had wandered around *Nashville* for about five days wondering what in the world this movie was going to be about. I mean, there were all these people, but how was I going to link them together? I went to this place called The Exit Inn. It was the only sort of "with-it" music place in *Nashville* at that time, which was 1973, I believe. Anyhow, I was sitting in the back and Jerry Jeff Walker was playing a song on stage. He was singing, "The words to this song don't mean anything at all."

There was a young woman who had taken too much of something and she was having convulsions. This black man came up and sat down and told me that he had just been released from prison for premeditated murder. He said that he'd gotten himself out by hiring thirteen lawyers. I said, "Oh, great." He kept talking to me and then he shook my hand and slid a joint up my sleeve. I thought, "Oh perfect," you know, "Now you're going to get arrested." But he was wonderful, because he told me about his life as an act of survival. He mentioned that he only slept a few hours each night because he had so much to make up for. He worked two shifts at the hospital and would come to The Exit Inn every night and listen to music. Suddenly, I thought, "This is exactly what the structure of this movie has to be about." That our lives are made up of simultaneous things happening that implode us with equal degrees of pain and pleasure all at the same time. At the time I was getting a divorce and my children were far away. I was feeling guilty about even being there, I mean a girl without a boy in a place where you go to hear music! So I realized that this would become the form of the film.

Q: *Has Robert Altman been helpful to you?*

A: I think the thing Altman did for me that was absolutely major was that he took me seriously. I was privy during the shooting of *McCabe and Mrs. Miller* to every single thing that went on, on a set. I was not kept away from anything, so I was allowed to have the experience go through me in my own time. He even said when I started to work for him that I should certainly take advantage of him because he would certainly take advantage of me — which is very true. He takes everyone's ideas, but that is part of working in a collaborative way, and I learned that film is collaborative. It is not about one person.

I also think that one of the great things about Bob is that he creates an atmosphere on a set that is really fun. Often in the film industry, it's not fun, in that the people on sets are so uptight about the rigors of budget that they forget about being sponta-neous. So those of us who worked with Bob were allowed a kind of freedom to laugh or try something that was a little different.

Q: *What was your first dramatic feature?*

A: *Old Boyfriends.* It was a Paul Schrader script. It had started out as a story about a man who went to look up all of his old girl-friends, and then the women's movement came along and he changed it and made it a girl going back. I felt she was going back to redefine herself in terms of looking at all these past loves in her life, that she had to do that before she could go any fur-ther into her future. I guess basically that's what it was, a woman's journey backwards so she could go forward.

Q: *Is the film reflective of a woman's point of view, even though a man wrote it?*

A: I've always felt very strongly that there is a point of view of the person. Yes, some women may write women brilliantly, but as in the old days of directing, there were some wonderful male directors who brought out certain qualities of women that I don't know if I could bring out of a woman. When I was asked the question very early in my career about the woman's point of view, it really used to make me angry. It seemed to put everything in a box. Everything has to be seen a certain way and that's not right. Each of us is individual. We all have our range of experiences, and that's what makes each soul unique. It's not just boy, girl, dog, cat. It's a voice that has been very carefully honed by certain experiences, and I think that to put it in a framework like a man's or woman's point of view sells everything very short. There are some young men who are going to have much more important things to say about women. I think of young men my son's age, twenty, twenty-two, he's been raised by a very different set of rules than men before, so he will have some very curious points of view about women, if he chooses to.

Q: *Do women in the business, executives at studios, have any real power in Hollywood? Do they use their power to give other women jobs?*

A: When you ask about women being in power, in positions of power, and is it easier now in Hollywood, I think it's much more open than it was, and more women are shooting films. But until a woman owns a film studio, until a woman comes with a hundred million dollars in her repertoire, I don't think it's going to be much easier at all. Because really, in this town, money is power. You have all these heads of studios and you have all these jobs that women have been slotted into, but they don't mean anything.

Q: *How has the opportunity for women to get that initial break changed since you started?*

A: I think that when I started there was Joan Darling, Joan Micklin Silver, Karen Arthur, myself, and for a brief moment Jane Wagner. The doors opened reluctantly and we all kind of rushed through at the same time. Then there was a tremendous setback around 1980 when the whole industry caved in on itself. I can't remember, but they went from making two hundred films a year to suddenly ninety seven movies being made. So there was this huge pulling back, and women were not employed at that particular time.

Joan Tewkesbury directing *The Acorn People*

There were too many men who were out there unemployed who got the jobs.

When Susan Seidelman did her film *Desperately Seeking Susan*, it opened the door for women. Also, in film schools and universities they are churning out just as many girls now as boys, so women have started to invade the territory. So it allows Joan Micklin Silver, Karen Arthur, Joan Darling, myself and Jane Wagner to re-enter on their coattails in a way. In Europe it's been a bit easier for women. They arrived at this place a lot sooner than we did. I think that when I started I very much wanted to be part of, or one of the boys. It was not about meeting boys and getting dates, it was about working with men, because men had the ability to go out in the world and get things accomplished. Women stayed at home. I'm fifty-one, so my whole frame of reference had to do with this certain kind of orderly life that you were supposed to maintain. That feeling hasn't changed until very recently. Again we go back to this thing where it's not either the boys or the girls or anything, it's people who are making decisions to work together. But I think that that was very important in the beginning, that you sort of took on this tomboy attitude about some of this stuff.

Q: *Has being a filmmaker meant making compromises to your life?*

A: I think that anyone in the film industry makes a compromise on another kind of life. The ramifications of choices that I made fifteen years ago are just making themselves present. I made a shift in my family. My children had their permanent home with their father and a stepmother. Probably if I were to look at it today, I wouldn't make that decision. I would figure out some other way to do it. But at the time it was the only way that I could do it. That was a tremendous sacrifice. Yet I'm not sorry. I can't deny the fact that I wish it were different, but it was the only thing that I could do at that moment in time.

So I think that in this industry — and again it has to do with changing ideas of the world — I think that no longer do men and women have these isolated roles. We don't think too much about it if men and women go off and do these larger than life kinds of experiences. People say, "That's great. He's going to China for a year and she's going to Afghanistan." It's a different kind of attitude about families than before. That is not to say that it's easier. Women are now into trying to have babies on their own at the last minute before nature's clock runs out. That is a very difficult decision. Women have to decide whether they can raise a family and be in this industry and make a living at it. And if you make a living at it, do you miss the growth of your children? Yes, sometimes you do. Those are hard things to choose.

Q: *Do you have problems on the set because you're a woman?*

A: I was in Texas and we were scouting locations in a van. I always sit in the back because I don't want to talk to anyone. I just want to look. The First A.D.[Assistant Director] was in the front seat. The teamsters in the front of the van started wondering, "Who the broad was that was gonna shoot the movie, and when was she gonna turn up, and what kind of person was this gonna be." They'd never worked with a woman director before. It went on for some time, until finally we stopped. We got out at the first location and he opened the door. This guy's standing there, and he sticks his hand out to help me out of the car. I said, "I'm the broad, and it's very nice to meet you." He was deeply embarrassed. He said, "We've never had a woman director before and we didn't know what to expect." He got very embarrassed. He was a Southern guy and he was still into opening doors and all that stuff. I told him, "Don't worry about a thing. It'll be fine." I've never had much problem with that. I guess mainly because I'm very bossy and it lets people know right away who's in charge.

Q: *How do you pitch a project?*

A: There's various forms of packaging. It's truly like setting up a real estate deal. Especially now because you have to have a major star attached to the property before you can go in and pitch it. Even independents who used to not care very much. So you find yourself gearing the story for various audiences. If you're going in to pitch to Sherry Lansing and Stanley Jaffe, you will address certain issues in the pitch. If you are going in to a young team that has had two hot movies at Warner Brothers, and now they're producers, you will find yourself doing a little razzamatazz. So you become the actor, and you sometimes find yourself having to perform all the parts. I was just in a situation where I went into a studio with two producers to pitch. One of them said, "Oh, I'll pitch it." I said, "Are you sure?" And he said, "Yes. It'll be just fine." Well he got in there and not being experienced in acting like those of us who are writers and actors, he fall apart. I said, "I'm sorry, I have to jump in right here." Then I proceeded to do my tap dance for the piece. It's like watching your audience and suddenly they're falling asleep and you've got to get them back alive again. It's about showmanship.

So it doesn't hurt to have had a little acting experience. Pitching has really come down to being an artform. Anyhow, hopefully it is an artform within a business, in that you take the rules of the game, and it is a game like any other game, like playing bridge where you see how many finesses you can make. It's a game. But when you sit at the table, or when you stand on the floor, that is where the artistry rises.

You also have to remember that if you've been beaten down by the business, which happens, you have to take these vacations.

I can't stay here all the time. I have to take trips. I have to either get in a car or go in a plane and go some place where I've never been before and just have it jolt me so that I forget about this stuff. Knowing that I'm not involved in all that other outside world stuff, I can climb back in and go back to work.

Q: *What are the benefits of working in television?*

A: I find that the cable stuff is so much easier to do as a rule. It's easier to get the projects going. The kind of projects that I want to do are the sort of stories and content that often doesn't appeal to a major studio. So some place like Turner, or Live Time, or HBO is a place where you can take these things, especially if you have a book that you want to adapt, and you can do the film.

Q: *Do you look for projects that are a tool for social change?*

A: Certainly the film *Unknown Soldier* has a lot to say about social change. I was doing rewrites during the time that Bush was giving his annual address about how great it was that we had gone to war a year ago. And it just fit very nicely in the Mayor's mouth. I mean we are in essence going back to that same bullshit about patriotism that is supposed to be like an opus, and I guess it was when everybody went off to war, but thank God everybody's turned around and said wait a minute that didn't work out so well. And then I did *Sudie and Simpson* for LiveTime and that is a film that was adapted from a book and it's about a child who is molested by a teacher at school. And I did a film last year for NBC with Dolly Parton in it called *Wild Texas Wind*. That was a story that Dolly had done. She commissioned a writer to do it. It's really about women being taken advantage of, physically abused, and that they let themselves in for it, the horror of that. And it's about a country and western singer and her manager.

Q: *What is it like working with a star on a project that they initiated?*

A: That was great. I don't take the job unless I'm like-minded with the people that I'm going to work with. Otherwise it's silly. You might as well just stay at home or pass on it. And so in the case of these projects I've been extremely like-minded with the producers and it's very important.

Q: *Is it easier, or getting easier for women to direct now?*

A: It doesn't make any difference I don't think. It's easier to direct and there are more women directing, but the kinds of things that you are asked to direct hasn't changed much. You have to be fairly self-motivated to try to get your own material done. There are not too many movies out there that are the *Sudie and Simpson's,* or exclusively women's stories. But there are situations where you can come in and at least add a point of view and a layer to it that nobody ever thought of before because you're directing it. And I think that there are a lot of women who are working in television, episodic and longer formats of television now, a lot more than before.

And so that part of it is somewhat encouraging. The thing that's not encouraging is the climate around these massively huge, costly pictures and the sensibility that goes with that. You don't get to direct any of those — and you may not want to. But there are exceptions. Randa Haines getting to do *The Doctor* was very important. I don't know how it did financially, but I think it did well enough. So she's in very good shape to press on. But it's slow going.

NINETEEN

Anne Wheeler

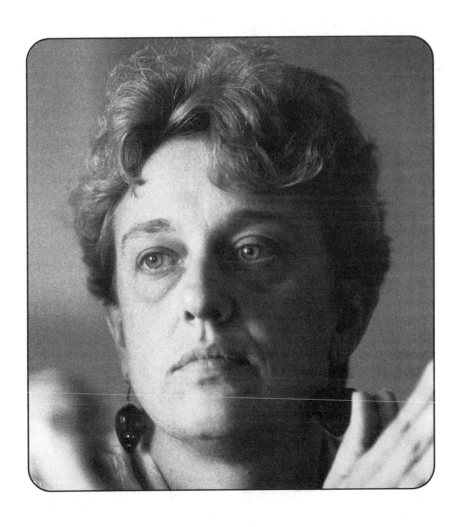

Filmography

Great Grandmother (1975), Documentary Short

Augusta, Priority: The Only Home I've Got (1978), Documentary Short

A War Story (1980), Docu-drama

A Change of Heart (1983) CBC TV

Loyalties (1985), Norstar Releasing

Cowboys Don't Cry (1986), CBC TV

Bye Bye Blues (1989), Allarcom/True Blue Films

Angel Square (1990), Atlantis Films

The Diviners (1993), Atlantis Films

One of Canada's leading filmmakers, Anne Wheeler recently made four feature films in nearly the same number of years — a rare accomplishment for anyone, let alone a woman based in the Northwest Canadian Prairies. Born and raised in Alberta, the forty-five-year-old native of Edmonton found her way into movies in the mid 1970s. She brought to her filmmaking the wide range of experiences from her vast background as a musician, teacher, mathematician, actress, photographer, and world traveler. As one of the founders of Film West, a Western Canadian film co-op, Wheeler learned the nuts and bolts of film production by trying her hand at all the technical positions. She fondly remembers shooting her very first film footage upside down. However, by clamping an inverted projector to a ceiling, she was still able to show the footage to an audience.

Her first film, *Great Grandmothers*, made in 1975, documents the history of prairie women. It won over ten major awards. Since then she has worked in various capacities on more than thirty films, most of them documentaries. Her highly acclaimed docu-drama, *A War Story*, is based on her father's World War II diaries while he was captive in a Japanese P.O.W. camp.

In 1983 she directed the CBC drama *A Change of Heart*, written by Alberta novelist Sharon Riis. Two years later, Wheeler released her first theatrical feature, *Loyalties*, also penned by Riis. Opening to rave reviews, the hard-hitting drama about sexual molestation secured her a reputation for handling sensitive and controversial material. A few years later, *Bye Bye Blues* caught the attention of critics. The film is based on her mother's life in Edmonton during World War II and is an epic by Canadian standards, costing $4.6 million dollars.

Wheeler has recently relocated to Saltspring Island, off the British Columbia coast, and continues to write and develop features from her new base.

Q: *Can you tell me your background as a filmmaker?*

A: I had a number of careers before I was a filmmaker, and I was dissatisfied with all of them. I was a mathematician, a high school teacher, and a photographer. I came back from a long, long trip around the world and a number of old friends of mine were starting to make films. They had absolutely no idea how to make films but they wanted to make films about the West, from the West. They wanted to interview me. I soon became more intrigued about what was happening on the other side of the camera than in front of the camera. They were all men, nine men I had known at university, and they were forming a collective. It was just the early 70s and a time when everybody felt they could do anything, and so we joined up and made a collective. It was a terrific way to learn how to make films because none of us even knew how to load a camera. We knew nothing.

We took turns being a director, a sound person, a camera person. The first time I went out to shoot I had to read a manual on how to run a camera. I was sent off by myself and I came back with four 100 foot rolls all shot, and I thought it was perfectly exposed. Then I discovered that I had held the camera upside down. But I guess we took the risks and we just did it as well as we could and learned from our mistakes and heaven knows we didn't make those kinds of mistakes twice.

When I first started, I only worked with men for the first three or four years and then I went through a period when I only worked with women. That was followed by a period where I did everything myself. I shot it, I edited it, I wrote it, I produced it. It sort of evolved from documentary into short dramas, and from short dramas into features.

Q: *Do you find being a woman filmmaker challenging?*

A: I haven't had any trouble working with men recently, but certainly I've gone through periods in my career where the problem has been partly within myself, lacking confidence and assuming that they know more than me. I sometimes ended up on a shoot where I would tell my cameraman to do something and he would argue with me as though I wasn't the director. I would immediately be intimidated instead of angry. And so it took a while to find the camera people who would respect me as a director. And of course sometimes the subjects that I've wanted to make films about have been difficult to get money for because I'm always going to men for money and they can't relate to the material. I guess a perfect example of that would be *Loyalties* where it was a story about a friendship between two women. I went to dozens and dozens of producers, including women producers, who thought a film about a friendship between two women was not commercial and was not going to sell. It was hard to find someone who was willing to raise the money for it and take the risk. I actually think that women in Canada have had considerable success directing features.

Q: *How would you describe your approach to directing?*

A: I think that people on a dramatic set, where there's fifty people, expect you to come on as a general, as a leader. My approach to dramatic direction is more motherly, as a person who tries to see that everybody on the crew and everybody in the cast does the best they can do. If everybody does their best, then you'll get the best film. And certainly with every crew, I usually go the set and people kind of look around and say, "Well gee, she's not much of a director. I mean, I can hardly hear her. Why isn't she taking over the situation?" I work sort of intimately; I go from person to person, whispering in people's ears, and my conversations are always one to one and very intimate. And it is not the role that a lot of people see a director taking. They see them going on to a set and yelling and screaming, and I find I don't get the best work out of people by taking that rather masculine position on a set. Also, I think, there is just a sense that women aren't leaders of great numbers of people, and that the stories that we want to tell aren't commercial. And the people who are putting the money into the film are often men or people who don't have the confidence in our stories. I think it's a tremendous undertaking to take on a feature film project, and a tremendous financial risk, and people are just not at the stage where they have the confidence in women directors yet.

Q: *What was it like when you first started in the film industry?*

A: Well, the first time I went on a set, or a crew, it was a documentary crew and I was a production assistant. Being my first time I tried to learn all the names; the Arriflex, the Nagra, all the names of the things. And it was a totally male crew. It was nine other guys, and I got into the van and they said, "Have you brought the dildo?" So I ran back and I went through the cupboards and I looked all over the place and nothing had the word "dildo" on it. And I came back very shamefaced and said, "I'm sorry... I can't find it." So one of them hopped out and ran in, and came back with something under his coat and leapt into the van and off we went. And so the next day I went down and charged through all the stuff trying to figure out what the dildo was and of course it was just a big joke. They thought I was a big joke, being a female on this crew, and it was a boy's club. So this went on for four days until finally someone took me aside and told me what a dildo was. For years we worked together and they would always ask me if I brought the dildo.

Q: *Why did you move from making documentaries to drama?*

A: I think I started directing drama because I had done a lot of documentaries and I had found myself in places where either I couldn't tell the truth because I felt I was going to exploit the people that were in the film, or I didn't want to put them through what I was going to have to put them through in order to say what I wanted to say. In particular, there was a film about my father being in a Japanese prisoner of war camp, and I was interviewing people who had gone through that hell for four, five, six years, and they were reliving these accounts. You could see that they wanted to do it because it was about my father, and they felt they maybe owed their lives to my father. But a lot of them confessed to me afterwards that they hadn't thought about it for years, and the interviews I did with them brought up all sorts of things within their lives that they found very emotional and very, very difficult to deal with. Also there were parts of *A War Story* that I couldn't talk about because there was no footage, there was no real way of putting an image to it, so I started to do docu-dramas where I would create, as close as I could, a sense of the footage that would

Anne Wheeler (second from right)
directing *Loyalties*

have been taken had it been a documentary film crew there at the moment. I slowly evolved from documentary into drama because there just wasn't enough documentary footage to say what I wanted to say.

Q: *Has anyone had an influence on your craft?*

A: Coming from a documentary film background, documentary filmmakers have influenced me as much as dramatic filmmakers. And being so far from a center, living in Edmonton, Alberta, I can't really pinpoint one film director that has really influenced me because I've really learned from trial and error, not from a study of any particular technique or approach to filmmaking. I love the intimacy of Bergman and I like the kind of spontaneity of Cassavetes. I've picked up from everybody, but I don't think I'm really inspired by one director.

Q: *Do you see your films as different than say a film made by a man?*

A: Well I try not to stereotype men and women as different kinds of filmmakers. I try to take them as individuals, and I think

I'm as different from Sandy Wilson as I am from many men. I think we have different stories we want to tell, and I think that we're very fortunate as women in this day and age making films because there are so many films that haven't been made because there haven't been the women to make them. So I think we have different stories to tell but I think our styles are as diverse as men's styles are diverse.

Q: *Do you enjoy working as an independent filmmaker?*

A: I guess one has a great sense of freedom and a sense of adventure. Having been on staff at the National Film Board and having been a freelancer, certainly I was richer as a staff person than I am as a freelancer. But things I initiate, I feel get rolling because I get out of them what I put into them. Whereas working for a large organization, like the Film Board, I never quite felt in control of what I was doing. It seemed like everybody else, or some other structure, was taking over my life. Now, I sit in my backyard and I write scripts for six or eight months, and then I put on a producer's hat and I go raise money to develop it. Then I write some more until it is a polished script and then I put my director's hat on and go looking for a producer. And so it's varied, and it's very much tailored to my own personality and my own lifestyle right now, which is raising two small children.

Q: *What is* Loyalties *about?*

A: *Loyalties* initially is about a friendship, a very unlikely friendship, between an upper class English woman and a Métis, that is a half-breed woman, who makes her living as a barmaid working in a local bar in a small northern Canadian town. But in fact, its about sexual child abuse and women having to stand together in order to combat this aggression towards our children.

So it's about the English woman, and her *Loyalties* toward her husband who she knows has sexually abused children in the past and she has covered for him. She makes a friendship with this woman whose child he rapes and the English woman has to decide whether she's going to stand beside her husband or with her new friend, her very unlikely friend, the Métis woman.

Q: *How did you handle the rape scene in* Loyalties?

A: The rape scene in *Loyalties* we kept until the last day of the shooting. And of course everybody was terrified of it. I was dreading it because I knew very clearly in my mind what I wanted, and the scene wasn't nice. I had long talks with the girl Diane who was playing Leona, about why I was doing it and why it was going to have to be awful and why she was going to have to go through this. This is a thirteen-year-old girl with a great maturity, and she understood completely. But I think Kenny Welsh, who of course was playing the doctor, was even more terrified. He was going to have to rape the child.

I went through great detail about everything that was going to happen and how he was going to have to rape this child physically. And we went on for about an hour before the set was ready, before we were all ready to go. I turned to him and I said, "Are you ready, Kenny?" And he turned to me and he said, "Yes, Mommy." And we just did it. It was like a first take.

Everybody had anticipated it for five weeks. What is it going to turn out like. We knew that this was the soul of the film. Everything really pivoted on these next few minutes of cinema. And he was so frightened because he had to lead the scene. I mean his aggression had to lead the scene. We all knew why we were doing it, and we got rid of almost everybody who was absolutely not necessary. The first take was perfect because they knew exactly why we were doing this.

Q: *Did you find* Loyalties *a rewarding experience?*

A: In *Loyalties*, I think I'm proud of the sense of reality that I was able to capture, especially within the Native households. Also representing a small prairie town in a very true light, in almost a documentary way so that the people in the film say, "Yes, that's true to life."

Q: *What are the qualities of a good director?*

A: I think passion is one quality, a belief in one's story. Essentially I'm a story teller in the old traditional sense of being a storyteller. I think a compassion and an understanding of human nature, because I think that as a film director you have to understand all the people that you're working for and that are with you, and understand what their needs are and try to see that those needs are fulfilled. It's not unlike being a good parent or a good friend or a good businessperson or a judge of character.

That's why I love it, because it is so eclectic. Everything that you've done in your life comes into play and helps you make a better movie.

TWENTY

Sandy Wilson

Filmography

Garbage (1969) Short

Penticton Profile (1970), Short, CFMDC

The Bridal Shower (1971), Short, CFMDC

He's Not the Walking Kind (1972), Short, CFMDC

Pen High Grad (1974), Short, CFMDC

Growing Up in Paradise (1977), Short, CFMDC

My American Cousin (1985), Spectra Films Release

Moving Day (1986), CBC TV

Mama's Gonna Buy You A Mockingbird (1986), CBC TV

American Boyfriends (1989), Alliance Releasing

Harmony Cats (1993), Ark Films Release

Sandy Wilson was born in 1947 in Penticton, British Columbia, and has been writing, directing, and producing films out of her home base in Vancouver since 1969. Her early work concentrated on personal documentaries as a form of self expression. The people in the first few films were often related to her. For example, her brother was the subject of *He's Not the Walking Kind.* Wilson also made a number of films using (16mm) home movie footage that her father shot when she was a child. Two memorable films that resulted during this time are *Bridal Shower* and *Growing Up in Paradise.* Since Wilson focused on stories from her own life during her formative years as a documentary filmmaker, it seems appropriate that her first dramatic feature film would be autobiographical.

My American Cousin is set in British Columbia's Okanagan Valley, in the year 1959. Based on Wilson's childhood memories, it is the story of a twelve-year-old girl coming of age. It took two years to raise the $1.5 million budget, but the tenacity paid off. Sandy's little gem of a film swept the 1986 Genie Awards (Canada's equivalent of the Oscars), garnering six trophies, including best picture, screenplay, and direction. Her Canadian success quickly spread to America. *My American Cousin* opened in New York to rave reviews. Sandy was suddenly a hit with the U.S. critics.

Los Angeles agents began pursuing her, but Wilson decided to stay in Vancouver rather than emigrate to Hollywood. It was not until four years later that Wilson released her next feature film, *American Boyfriends,* a sequel to *My American Cousin.* This time the reception wasn't as warm as it had been with her debut. The film received poor reviews. It opened and closed as rapidly as her previous success had fallen upon her. Many people said it was too late for her to have made a sequel. Others said that audiences had shifted in taste, and were no longer interested in nostalgic coming of age pictures. Whatever the reason, Wilson takes it in stride, as she enthusiastically pursues her next pictures.

Q: *Can you tell me about your background and how you got into filmmaking?*

A: I got into filmmaking by chance. It had never crossed my mind to be a filmmaker. Then, when I as a student at Simon Fraser University, studying English and History, I took a filmmaking class and immediately got hooked on the image. I liked the accessibility to people and that process of putting the film together once you've shot your footage. I made a little ten minute film called *Garbage* and that was shown on the CBC. So I got a little taste of what it was like to have your films viewed by an audience. And then things just kept landing in my lap. It wasn't a conscious decision; in fact, I'm very surprised that I've continued making films.

Q: *Do you find it difficult working in this industry as a woman filmmaker?*

A: I think it's a little bit tough, because a lot of the power, and the money, and the control is watched over by men. And a lot of those men don't yet feel comfortable in dealing with a woman on an equal footing. They're far more used to having women as images up on the screen — as actresses, or secretaries, or wives. People they can either dismiss or divorce. If it doesn't go well, they can close the door and they'll be gone. So in that regard it's a little difficult to find men who enjoy working with women, and with that different energy level and commitment that many women have. But on the positive side of things, I think it's the women who have the stories that come from the heart, and it's the women who are very committed and won't be stopped. I think women have a terrific sense of humor and we've always told stories among ourselves. Maybe we haven't had quite as much self-confidence as we'd like to have in telling our stories to a wider audience, but I think that's changing. And I think also there are probably more men around now who enjoy working with women. So I remain optimistic.

Q: *Can you tell me the story of how you came upon the idea for* My American Cousin?

A: Whew! *My American Cousin . . .* It really began back in 1972 when I made a documentary about my handicapped brother Brian for the National Film Board. I included a little three minute clip in it based on my Dad's 16 millimeter home movies of us kids growing up at Paradise Ranch. And the response to that little three minute clip in *He's Not the Walking Kind* was so positive that I made a film from my Dad's 16 millimeter home movies. I called it *Growing Up in Paradise*. Again the response was very gratifying.

People found the film interesting and charming, and it spoke to them. So it seemed like a good idea to keep telling stories that I knew something about, stories from my past. And then I was up in the Okanagan one summer, and I heard a song on the radio. It was Johnny Horton singing the Ballad of New Orleans — "Well he ran through the bush and he ran through the brambles" — and it twigged in my mind the memory of this wonderful, gorgeous, fabulous boy who had arrived at the ranch in the middle of a hot, still summer night. My parents were very English and nothing was ever supposed to happen between nine o'clock at night and six o'clock in the morning. All of a sudden, in the middle of the night, this beautiful boy arrived and turned everything around, upside down. He had a fabulous white convertible which was chopped and channeled. He was so exciting I couldn't believe that we were even related to him. And then he was gone in a cloud of dust. I thought, this would make a nice movie because you've got the boy, the girl, the car, and that wonderful age of innocence back in 1959. It's the documentary side of me that's interested in how times have changed, and I thought it would be possible to capture that innocence, what it was like to be a girl, finding out about boys back in the Okanagan Valley in 1959.

So I immediately started on an outline, and in that same week I also got pregnant. I had a classic female dilemma on my hands. You start out on a film and you think, "Oh, a couple of months to write the script and get the financing and then we'll be shooting it next summer, right?" And I thought, "Gee, I'll have this little baby, I just don't know if I can do all this." But I thought, "Oh well, what the heck, go for it."

Q: *How did you raise the financing for* My American Cousin?

A: I went on a trip to Toronto and started pitching the project. I did a lot of what I call "dining for dollars," where I would talk to anyone who had money. That was a very interesting process because I had to learn how to talk with people who had money. I have nothing in my background that prepared me for any of that. There was a lot of pitching, talking to people — talking to anyone actually — in bars, on airplanes. . . friends and relations. It took two years to get the picture ready to go in front of the camera. To me it was a little bit like being pregnant and having a baby. When you're pregnant all you can think about is, "Oh my God, what is the delivery going to be like?" And you don't really think too much about having this little baby for the rest of your life, and what's your life going to be like on a 9-5 basis once you've got the kid. Then Peter O'Brian got involved. It happened through Phil. Phil Borsos and I are childhood friends. We both spent some time in Merrimack when we were kids. I bumped into Phil and he said, "I liked your script, can I show it to Peter?" Peter was busy, he had a whole lot of other projects, and so he said, "Thanks but no thanks, my plate is full." Then as fate would have it, he had to pull the plug on *One Magic Christmas* when it was ready to go. So all of a sudden he was looking for a picture.

Q: *Did financing the picture become a full time commitment?*

A: Yes! It become an obsession. The film became a real obsession with me. I knew it intimately, I could see it finished. And there has always been a special feeling about *My American Cousin*. When I would tell people about it they would seem to be interested. So I'd think, "I know there's an audience out there if only I could get this film made." You can see it made, and you keep going towards it.

Q: *What was your first day like on the set of the picture?*

A: The first day of the shoot, for me, was such a celebration. I've always been in filmmaking for the fun of it. I love making films. So I thought, "The first day of the shoot. God, its gonna be great!" I had a big discussion with myself. What am I gonna wear, so that everybody understands that you're the director, you're the person directing this picture. I figured that one out. So when I arrived on set, my first A.D. [Assistant Director] said, "Would you like a

Sandy Wilson on the set of *Mama's Gonna Buy You a Mockingbird.*

binder?" And I said, "What for?" And he said, "Well, to put your script in." I said, "I've written the script, I know the script. What do I need the script for?" This is from documentaries where you don't go out with a script. And he said, "Well, okay," and let it go at that. So, for the first day of the shoot I went out with just a little purse. All it contained was lipstick, the hotel key, and cab fare home. No script.

Next, my cameraman Richard Leiterman says to me, "Sandy, can I see your shot list?" I replied, "You mean my story board?" Because I did have a story board back at the motel. He said, "No Sandy, I mean your shot list." And I said, "You know, I've heard a lot about shot lists but I don't know exactly what they are." So there I am out on the first day of the shoot, "Hi guys, here we are." Richard Leiterman carried me for that day. The second day I started to get a little bit nervous because I realized that there was a great deal of work to the whole process. And then the third day was total blind terror because I thought, "This is too much, this is really too much." I learned very quickly how to do my shot list, how to do my homework. I carried my script with me. I put it in a big red binder — that became the bible. I felt naked without it. So, I went into it with this wonderful feeling, then within three days I was completely terrified. I took a few days to figure out what I was supposed to do as the director. And then we started to really cook. I loved it. It's a wonderful thing when everybody is contributing their very best. Film is such a collaborative thing, that everybody has to give you a hundred and fifty percent of themselves in order to make the whole greater than the sum of the parts.

Q: *Have you ever considered going south of the border?*

A: I've thought of working in Los Angeles. I would love to work in Los Angeles. I'd love to work in America. I'd love to work with Americans. They've got a terrific sense of energy and confidence and they do things quickly, as opposed to up here in Canada where we consider and write letters, and it goes to a committee, and you have to wait. So that American energy and momentum I find exciting. But I am a mother with two small boys and I'm very much rooted in Vancouver. I've got this wonderful support network all in place. So I would prefer to stay in Vancouver.

Q: *Have you made any personal sacrifices along the way in order to make films?*

A: To the heart of the matter. Well, my marriage fell apart. That was partly to do with how some men find it difficult to deal with a woman who's very successful, and straight-forward, and obsessed with her work. So that's something that you lose. I haven't had much of a social life, so I might have lost something there. I think almost all working mothers feel a little bit guilty that they should be spending more time with their children, or giving their children more of themselves. I try to balance that out and not feel so guilty about it any more. I remember weeping a lot in the course of making *My American Cousin*. There were some very, very difficult times.

Q: *What qualities make a good director?*

A: Well, I think a good director has to have a vision of the film that he or she wants to make. And they need to have the ability to communicate that vision to all of the people working on the film. I found most of the time that people want the director to be good, they want the director to tell them what to do. They want them to direct. And most of the crews that I've worked with — male, female, or whatever — they'll give you the benefit of the doubt. If you do know what you want, and can tell them what you want, they'll go to the wall for you.

Q: *Are you a director who likes to collaborate?*

A: It's funny, because I consider myself to be like a dictator/ doormat/director. I like to listen to what everybody has to say. Anyone. The people in the elevator, the caterers, the grips, the gaffers. I want to know what they think about my script, what they think about the casting. I want to know the far end of everything. But, I want to reserve the final decision for moi!